Decision Theory and Incomplete Knowledge

Z. W. KMIETOWICZ
and
A. D. PEARMAN

University of Leeds

Gower

Published by
Gower Publishing Company Limited,
Gower House, Croft Road, Aldershot,
Hampshire GU11 3HR, England.

British Library Cataloguing in Publication Data

Kmietowicz, Z.W.
Decision theory and incomplete knowledge.
1. Statistical decision
I. Title   II. Pearman, A. D.
519.5'42   QA279.4

ISBN 0-566-00327-9

1719762

Contents

Figures and tables

Preface

The approach to decision making presented in this book has been developed
by us over a number of years. Although the starting point for our work
was a problem often faced by businessmen or managers, the methods
described here are applicable to any decision situation in which the
future is uncertain and information about it limited. Some of the ideas
discussed in the book have appeared before in a variety of journals and
conference papers, while others are presented here for the first time.
They have been brought together in order to make them more readily
accessible to the general reader. This publication has enabled us to
present the material in a more systematic, comprehensive and, we trust,
lucid manner. Several detailed examples illustrating applications of
the methodology developed in the book are included in order to make
easier the assimilation of the material. This should help readers with
a limited mathematical background, and those interested primarily in
the more applied aspects of the subject.

Several people have helped us significantly in the development of the
methodology presented here and we would like to record our debt to them.
First is C.M.Cannon, now of the University of Kent, but previously a
colleague in the School of Economic Studies at the University of Leeds,
who was initially involved with Z.W.Kmietowicz in deriving some of the
basic results given in chapter three. Professor R.E.Alsop of the
Transport Studies Unit, University College, London drew attention to an
inadequacy in our original proof involving the derivation of the maximum
variance which was ultimately corrected by Dr. C.C.Agunwamba of the
University of Nsukka, Nigeria. Professor P.C.Fishburn of Pennsylvania
State University initially provided the suggestion of pairwise comparison
which led to the development of the material on weak statistical
dominance, and Dr. M.J.Ryan of the University of Hull was the first to
draw to our attention the possibility of using strong ranking of
probabilities of states of nature and of viewing our decision problem as
a constrained game against nature.

Like many authors, we have found that the preparation of a manuscript
for publication can only be undertaken with the active support and
encouragement of others. The help and consideration given by our
respective wives and families is greatly appreciated. So too is the
great care and attention which Jill Dunham has given to the preparation
of the final typescript. To her, and to everybody who has contributed
to the writing of this book, we should like to extend our thanks.

1 Introduction

One of the principal concerns of decision theory is with the development of analytical techniques for guiding the choice of a single course of action from among a series of alternatives, in order to accomplish a designated goal. It is an area where currently a great deal of work is being undertaken, some highly theoretical, but much of it concerned with the day-to-day decision making of business firms, government departments, nationalised industries, and similar organisations. As a result, an increasingly sophisticated range of tools is becoming available to enable the decision maker to use the information at his disposal in the most efficient way possible.

In decision theory, it is often useful to characterise the decision making process as a sequential series of component problems. It would be quite wrong to imply that the resulting framework is adequate for the analysis of all decision problems. Nevertheless, it is a useful device for highlighting the basic elements of decision making, and for providing a frame of reference. The first steps are:
- (1) Identify a set of mutually exclusive and collectively exhaustive alternative strategies which may be adopted.
- (2) Identify a set of mutually exclusive and collectively exhaustive alternative states of the world, in one of which the chosen strategy will have to operate.
- (3) Predict and evaluate the outcome of every possible strategy in every state of the world.

Undertaking these three steps yields $S_i (i = 1 \ldots m)$, which correspond to the alternative strategies identified in step (1), $N_j (j = 1 \ldots n)$ which are the states of the world (often termed states of nature) identified in step (2), and X_{ij} which correspond to the evaluation of the outcome of strategy i should state of nature j in fact occur.

Following the completion of the first three steps of the decision process, two further steps are required:
- (4) Form a view of the probabilities of occurrence of the different states of nature. This view may vary from an exact specification of probabilities, P_j, for each state of nature, at one extreme, to a statement that no sensible estimates of probabilities can be made, at the other.
- (5) Select a criterion by which to evaluate each strategy, and hence identify the one which performs best.

The framework just outlined may be used to describe either a single decision problem, or each stage of a dynamic problem where both the $\{S_i\}$ and $\{N_j\}$ sets may vary, depending upon the way in which the problem unfolds. A number of examples can be given to illustrate the kinds of problem which may be examined in this way.

Capital Investment A firm must decide which of a number of mutually exclusive investments to undertake. The feasible investments are represented by the $\{S_i\}$. The states of nature, $\{N_j\}$, might correspond to alternative sets of assumptions about the level of demand, raw material prices, wage negotiations, etc. For each combination an X_{ij}, probably representing the net present value of the investment to the firm, is computed.

Marketing   A marketing manager must decide which launching strategy to adopt for a new product. Different strategies $\{S_i\}$ might correspond to whether to launch the product nationally, or just in selected areas, whether to concentrate on television or newspaper advertising, and so on. The states of nature $\{N_j\}$ might represent alternative possibilities about public reaction to the product, state of the national economy, etc. For each combination an X_{ij} corresponding to the firm's resulting profit or loss can be calculated.

Medical Care   A doctor must decide on what course of action, i.e. what form of treatment, to offer to a patient with a given set of symptoms. States of nature correspond to different types of illness which the patient may, in fact, have and X_{ij} to, say, life expectancy.

Investment Portfolios   An investor must decide on the most appropriate way to allocate his funds. In this case, the strategies correspond to different investment mixes between equities, government stocks, property, etc. States of nature correspond to different future states of the market, and the X_{ij} to the net profit which can be anticipated for different mixes in different situations.

Agriculture   A farmer must decide about different combinations of fertilisers and crops that he might adopt. $\{S_i\}$ represent the alternative combinations, and the $\{N_j\}$ the different combinations of weather, market prices, etc. which may arise. The X_{ij} might be measures of crop yields, or of net financial benefit.

In this book, the emphasis will be on the fourth and fifth steps of the decision making model described earlier. More particularly, the matrix $\{X_{ij}\}$ will usually be taken as given, and attention will be focussed on how a choice of strategy may be made, and how the nature of the choice depends upon the kind of assessment of probabilities of future states of nature which the decision maker feels able to specify. Techniques for the assessment of probabilities will not themselves be treated in any great detail. What will prove crucial is the precision of the assessment that can be made.

In conventional decision theory, it is normal to identify two extreme cases in terms of the kind of assessment of probabilities which is possible. The first of these is the situation where the decision maker feels unable to make any statement about the vector of probabilities $\{P_j\}$ of the states of nature. Following the terminology initially suggested by Knight (1921), this is termed decision making under uncertainty. The second and opposite extreme corresponds to the decision maker being able to specify exactly values for all P_j such that the basic requirements $\sum_{j=1}^{n} P_j = 1$ and $\{P_j\} \geqslant 0$ are met. Knight termed this decision making under risk. For both decision making under risk and under uncertainty a series of well-established strategy choice rules exist. Under risk, maximisation of the expected value of the payoffs is typically used. Under uncertainty, a series of rules, such as maximax, maximin, or minimax regret, based on the extreme payoffs of strategies are available.

A more detailed account of decision making under risk and under uncertainty is given in chapter 2. However, the principal concern of this book is not with either of these extremes. This is because in many practical decision problems, the nature of the decision maker's beliefs about $\{P_j\}$ lies somewhere between the two extremes. Many real problems, therefore, may be classified as decision making under conditions of incomplete knowledge, a term due to Cannon and Kmietowicz (1974). Despite this fact, however, there has, until recently, been a notable lack of operational techniques for guiding decision making in such circumstances.

One of the first to investigate decision making under conditions of incomplete knowledge was Fishburn (1964). He suggested that a particularly realistic compromise between the extremes of uncertainty and risk, was to assume that the decision maker was able to rank future states of nature in terms of their probabilities, such that $P_1 \geqslant P_2 \ldots \geqslant P_n$. Although this was a very realistic assumption, as is explained in chapter 3, he did not pursue this approach very far.

In this book it will be shown how it is, in fact, possible to develop a rich variety of formal decision making models based on the assumption that decision makers are able only to rank the probabilities of future states of nature. Moreover, these techniques are, for the most part, very straightforward in their application. In chapter 2 a summary is given of the various branches of established decision theory, but with particular emphasis on the classical models of decision making under uncertainty. Some discussion of utility theory and its implications for decision making is included. Chapter 3 discusses Fishburn's results for decision making with ranked probabilities. It then goes on to explain why these results are quite severely restricted in their application. As a consequence, a new technique is developed, using limiting expected payoffs of strategies, based on the application of classical decision making under uncertainty criteria, but incorporating the ranking of P_j. It is demonstrated that not only is this approach more realistic, but it is also very straightforward in its application. The basic proofs depend upon a transformation of variables and the use of standard linear programming concepts, but application is a matter of simple arithmetic.

In chapter 4, it is argued that, in addition to expected values, the variance of the payoffs of a strategy is also a potential aid to decision making. Given only ranked P_j, it is impossible, to make any exact statement about strategy variance, but it is possible to calculate a maximum variance for each strategy. The theoretical derivations depend in this case on the solution of a quadratic programming problem, but, again, implementation needs no more than basic arithmetic. Given that both an expected value and a variance based assessment of strategies is available, the question addressed in chapter 5 is the simultaneous use of both in decision making. Circumstances in which decision makers may wish to trade off one against the other are discussed and a number of possible ways of doing this are examined.

In practical decision making, it is crucial to be aware of potential inaccuracies in the information which is contained in the specification of the states of nature, the corresponding $\{P_j\}$ vector, and also in the $\{X_{ij}\}$ matrix. Chapter 6, therefore, examines how sensitive strategy recommendation based on the methods discussed in chapters 3 and 4 is likely to be to changes in the underlying assumptions on which the initial decisions were made. This includes changes in the ranking of states of nature, introduction of new states of nature and changes in the payoff matrix. Further extensions of the basic results are contained in chapter 7. Among them are the possibility of using a Bayesian approach to updating the decision maker's current ranking of probabilities of states of nature in the light of experimental evidence, and also an assessment of the use of entropy as a measure of uncertainty, especially the implications of ranked probabilities for entropy based measures.

Chapters 8 and 9 deal in more detail with two particular extensions of the basic ideas for decision making with ranked probabilities. Chapter 8 develops a concept of 'weak' statistical dominance and contrasts it with Fishburn's 'strict' dominance, which happens to be a special case of the more general weak dominance result. This criterion enables pairs of strategies to be compared in circumstances less restrictive than those required for the application of Fishburn's results. Chapter 9 takes as its starting point work by Ryan (1976) and shows how the basic approach of chapter 3 can be embedded in the framework of a constrained game against nature, thus removing the assumption implicit in the original model that decision makers should adopt a pure strategy against nature. Some of the results obtained in chapter 3 are shown to be special cases of the more general results presented in this chapter.

Chapter 10, is concerned with examples of the application of a similar mathematical method to that used in earlier chapters to the problem of social choice incorporating individuals' preference rankings and to multiple criteria decision making. A short concluding chapter follows summarising the principal results and the main strengths and weaknesses of the methods described. It also suggests areas for further research.

2 Established techniques in decision making

2.1 INTRODUCTION

The aim of this chapter is to give a brief account of the main models used in decision making and to stress particularly decision making under uncertainty. General characteristics of a decision problem are discussed first; then a distinction is made between decision making under uncertainty and under risk and models appropriate for each situation are described. Decision problems intermediate between uncertainty and risk are also identified and their importance stressed. A discussion of the relationship between monetary payoffs and their utility equivalents concludes the chapter.

2.2 THE FRAMEWORK OF A DECISION PROBLEM

The classical decision model assumes that a decision maker can select one of a number of courses of action (strategies) open to him S_i, $i = 1, 2....m$. As the future is uncertain, the selected strategy must operate under one of a number of mutually exclusive and exhaustive states of nature, N_j, $j = 1, 2....n$. The eventual outcome or payoff of the selected strategy will depend on the state of nature which happens to arise. The payoff of strategy S_i given state of nature N_j is designated as X_{ij}. Thus the essential information of a decision problem may be conveniently summarised in a payoff matrix, as shown in Figure 2.1.

Strategy	State of Nature					
	N_1	N_2	$\cdots$	N_j	$\cdots$	N_n
S_1	X_{11}	X_{12}	$\cdots$	X_{1j}	$\cdots$	X_{1n}
S_2	X_{21}	X_{22}	$\cdots$	X_{2j}	$\cdots$	X_{2n}
.	.	.		.		.
.	.	.		.		.
S_i	X_{i1}	X_{i2}	$\cdots$	X_{ij}	$\cdots$	X_{in}
.	.	.		.		.
.	.	.		.		.
S_m	X_{m1}	X_{m2}	$\cdots$	X_{mj}	$\cdots$	X_{mn}

Figure 2.1: A Payoff Matrix

As an example, the reader may like to consider an investment problem where strategies correspond to a number of investment projects which a managing director may be considering. States of nature represent different economic conditions which may arise in the future, e.g. boom, slump, no change, while the payoffs represent evaluations of the strategies under different economic conditions. In this case payoffs could be rates of return on capital invested, profits if the amount of money invested in each project was the same, etc.

Several important assumptions underlie the characteristics of the decision problem summarised in Figure 2.1. The number of strategies available to a decision maker may in practice be larger than m and can sometimes be infinite e.g. as in the investment portfolio selection problem where each different mix of the shares held constitutes a different strategy. It is assumed, however, that the decision maker can eliminate many of them because they are inferior to one or more of the retained strategies, and that, even if in theory an infinite range of non-dominated strategies may be available, in practice the decision maker will analyse only a finite number.

Similar difficulties arise with the states of nature. Their number can again be infinite, e.g. when they represent the level of economic activity. Considerations of economy and expediency demand, however, that their number be kept low, either excluding those which are unlikely to occur, or by defining them more broadly, e.g. economic conditions may be described as favourable, neutral or unfavourable. It is also necessary to specify them in such a way that the occurrence of one excludes the others. Another implicit assumption is that the action of the decision maker has no influence on the states of nature. This would not be so, for example, if a decision maker was considering a large investment in manufacturing capacity which could have a significant effect on the level of economic activity. It is also assumed that nature does not respond in any way which depends upon the strategy selected by the decision maker, i.e. it neither hinders him nor helps him consciously. If, for example, the probability of occurrence of states of nature can be influenced by an opponent of the decision maker, then classical decision theory does not apply and recourse has to be made to the theory of games.

Evaluation of payoffs also presents difficulties. It is usually assumed that they are single-valued. In most cases, however, a combination of a strategy and a state of nature, especially if it is broadly defined, can result in a variety of payoffs, although it is assumed that their variability is not too great. They are best viewed as random variables, which are represented by a single value, e.g. the average, in order to simplify the problem. This restrictive assumption is relaxed somewhat in chapter 6.

2.3 THREE APPROACHES TO DECISION MAKING

The framework of the decision problem described in section 2.2 forms a common starting point for three approaches to decision making, which are distinguished by the amount of information they assume to be available about the probabilities with which the states of nature are likely to occur. The first approach assumes that the decision maker is working in conditions of complete uncertainty about the future, i.e., that no information about the probabilities is available to him. Following the distinction made by Knight (1921) this situation is referred to as decision making under uncertainty.

The second approach takes the view that probabilities of the states of nature can be specified uniquely, either by repeated experimentation (where this is possible) or by eliciting unique subjective probabilities from the decision maker. Knight termed this decision making under conditions of risk.

The third approach attempts to strike a balance between the two approaches mentioned above. It assumes that in many decision problems (particularly in business) some information is available about the probabilities of the states of nature, but that it is not comprehensive enough to enable exact specification of the probabilities. Decision making in such circumstances is referred to as decision making under conditions of incomplete knowledge. This problem is the main concern of this book. Before discussing the problem in greater detail, however, it is advisable to describe decision making under conditions of uncertainty and under risk in greater detail because they constitute the two limiting cases from which the third approach was developed.

2.4 DECISION MAKING UNDER UNCERTAINTY

In this case it is assumed that the decision maker has no information about the probabilities of the states of nature. Such a situation is often postulated when investment decisions are considered. Many such decisions are unique and past experience is of little help in trying to predict how likely are the relevant states of nature. Moreover, success or failure of investment decisions often depends on the performance of the whole economy which can be blown off course by unforeseen developments like a major strike, political uncertainty or shortage of energy.

In spite of the difficulties, decisions have to be made. Several criteria have been proposed to help decision makers facing such conditions.

The maximin criterion suggests that the decision maker should examine only the minimum payoffs of strategies and select the strategy with the largest of these, hence the name. This criterion is very attractive to a cautious decision maker who wants to ensure that even if an unfavourable state of nature occurs, there is a known minimum payoff below which he cannot fall. Such an approach may well be justified because the minimum payoffs may have high probability of occurrence, although this is not known, or because realisation of a very low payoff may lead to financial ruin.

The maximax criterion adopts just the opposite viewpoint. It advises the decision maker to examine only maximum payoffs of strategies and to select the strategy with the largest of these. The criterion reflects the viewpoint of a very optimistic decision maker who is greatly attracted by the high payoffs and who hopes that the uncertain future develops favourably for him. The criterion may also appeal to a decision maker who likes to gamble and who is sufficiently wealthy to be able to write off the losses, when they occur, without suffering undue inconvenience.

The Hurwicz criterion attempts to strike a balance between the two approaches mentioned above. It suggests that the minimum and maximum payoffs of each strategy should be averaged using as weights α and $1 - \alpha$, where α is the index of pessimism, and the strategy with the highest average selected. The index α reflects the decision maker's attitude to risk taking. An extremely cautious decision maker will set $\alpha = 1$ and then the Hurwicz criterion reduces to the maximin criterion. When $\alpha = 0$ we have the case of the extremely optimistic decision maker using the maximax criterion.

The minimax 'regret' criterion looks at the regret, opportunity cost or loss which arises when a particular state of nature is assumed to have occurred and the payoff of the selected strategy is smaller than the maximum payoff which could have been attained for that state of nature. The regret corresponding to a particular payoff X_{ij} is defined as $R_{ij} = X_j(\text{max}) - X_{ij}$ where $X_j(\text{max})$ is the maximum payoff attainable under the state of nature N_j. This definition of regret enables the decision maker to transform the payoff matrix into a regret matrix and the minimax criterion suggests that he should look at the maximum regret of each strategy and select the one with the smallest of these. The criterion takes the viewpoint of a cautious decision maker who wants to ensure that the selected strategy does well in comparison with other strategies irrespective of which state of nature happens to arise. It is particularly attractive to a decision maker who knows that several of his competitors face identical or very similar problems and who is aware that his performance will be evaluated in relation to the attainments of his competitors. Such a situation often arises when several branch managers of the same company make commercial decisions in almost identical circumstances and whose performance is evaluated not in isolation but in relation to the other branch managers.

The Bayes-Laplace criterion employs the principle of insufficient reason which postulates that if no information is available about the probabilities of the states of nature, it is only reasonable to assume that they are equally likely. Thus, if there are n states of nature, the probability of each is $1/_n$. The criterion goes on to suggest that the decision maker should calculate expected payoff for each strategy and select the one with the highest of these. The use of expected values distinguishes this criterion from the other complete ignorance criteria which utilise only extreme payoffs of strategies. This feature makes the criterion similar to decision making under risk, which is discussed in the following section.

A notable disadvantage of the complete ignorance criteria (with exception of the Bayes-Laplace criterion) is their exclusive reliance on the extreme payoffs of strategies. The intermediate payoffs may well be quite numerous and, taken jointly, more likely than the extreme payoffs. Obviously, they should play a role in the decision making process. This is particularly true when the extreme payoffs of strategies do not differ very much. A more fundamental criticism of the complete ignorance criteria concerns the validity of the assumption of total lack of information about the probabilities with which the states of nature are likely to occur. In many situations, particularly in business and industry, the decision maker will be fairly confident that certain states of nature are much more likely than others, e.g., the current performance of the economy and economic forecasts made by government and independent agencies may give a strong indication that over the next few years favourable conditions are much more likely than unfavourable ones. However imprecise is such information, it seems very unwise to ignore it completely.

2.5 DECISION MAKING UNDER RISK

In decision making under risk it is assumed that exact probabilities of the states of nature are available. Sometimes, the probabilities can be established experimentally or deduced from a priori considerations; on other occasions the decision maker's subjective probabilities are used. In the latter case, the probabilities are based on the decision maker's beliefs about the future, and are obtained from him directly or indirectly in a number of ways, see section 2.6. This is invariably the case with decision making in business where experimentation is impossible. Once the probabilities of the states of nature are established, it is natural to calculate expected payoffs for strategies, and to use this index of each strategy's performance as a major determinant of strategy choice.

An important advantage of a maximum expected value criterion is the utilisation of the probabilities of the states of nature and of all the payoffs of strategies. This approach to decision making does not exclude the possibility that another strategy may be preferable to the selected one under some states of nature, but it ensures that if many similar decisions are taken (payoffs and probabilities may change from problem to problem), the decision maker will do better in the long run than if he had employed a complete ignorance criterion.

A major criticism of the maximum expected value criterion is its unsuitability for unique and important decisions. Here the worst outcome of the selected strategy (if it occurs) may well ruin the decision maker financially, and it is no consolation to him to know that the strategy also contains a number of very attractive outcomes. Moreover, if a particular decision can ruin him, there will be no possibility of offsetting the loss in the long run. Even if the loss can be sustained, it may be very difficult and may take a long time to make it up.

Another criticism of the expected value criterion concerns the determination of the subjective probabilities of states of nature. It is argued that in many decision problems the decision maker is unable to specify the probabilities with any accuracy because a lot of uncertainty invariably surrounds future events. This particular difficulty is discussed further in the following section.

2.6 ESTIMATION OF SUBJECTIVE A PRIORI PROBABILITIES

One attempt to deal with the difficulty of obtaining exact subjective probabilities of states of nature is due to Savage (1954). Other approaches are described in, e.g., Raiffa, (1968); Hampton et al (1973);

or Moore and Thomas (1975). Savage argued that, even if the decision maker is unable to specify exactly his subjective probabilities, deep down in his subconscious such a set must exist, and it is only necessary to elicit it from him. He suggested that this may be done by asking him a series of hypothetical questions about the probabilities of the states of nature, e.g. is P_1 larger than P_3, or $P_1 + P_2$ larger than $P_3 + P_4$, etc. The replies can be analysed with the help of the laws governing probabilities, and an exact set of probabilities estimated. Such experiments have, in fact, been conducted, but unfortunately it soon became apparent that the replies were often inconsistent. The greater the uncertainty about the future the greater was the number of inconsistent replies. These experiments seem to suggest that decision makers have some useful information about probabilities of states of nature, but it is not sufficiently detailed to ensure a unique specification. Another criticism of Savage's procedure is that answers provided by decision makers to hypothetical questions may not quite correspond to their perception of the situation in a real life decision problem. Moreover, the procedure is rather cumbersome, time-consuming and costly. Much the same criticisms apply to all probability elicitation techniques.

2.7 MONETARY AND UTILITY PAYOFFS

So far it has been assumed that entries in the payoff matrix are specified in terms of money or some other objective scale common to all decision makers, e.g., market share, rate of return, etc. It has also been implied that frequently these payoffs do not correspond to the decision maker's valuation of certain outcomes. This is often the case with business decisions. For example, one payoff may show a small loss and another a small profit. In money terms the difference between the two may be small, but their attractiveness to the decision maker may differ greatly, because the first may lead to commercial collapse while the second may mean survival.

When monetary payoffs do not correspond directly to decision maker's subjective valuations, it is possible to convert them into utilities with the help of a suitable utility function, e.g., when the marginal utility of money diminishes as its quantity increases, a simple assumption is that utility is an appropriate function of the logarithm of money. Having replaced monetary payoffs by their subjective utilities, the decision maker can employ any of the complete ignorance criteria to select a strategy if no information about the probabilities of states of nature is available, or use expected utility (perhaps in conjunction with standard deviation) when the probabilities are available.

An alternative method of determining subjective probabilities of individual payoffs is to use the utility theory developed by von Neumann and Morgenstern (1947). It is based on a number of generally acceptable axioms concerning decision maker's consistency of preferences between various payoffs. An important result of the theory is that the utility of a lottery (gamble), which offers two payoffs, X_1 and X_2, with probabilities p and 1 - p respectively, is equal to the expected value of the utilities of the two outcomes,

$$U = pU(X_1) + (1-p) U(X_2) \qquad (2.1)$$

where $U(X_1)$ and $U(X_2)$ are the subjective utilities of the two payoffs. Moreover, if the decision maker is indifferent between the lottery given in (2.1) and another payoff, X_{ij}, which lies between X_1 and X_2 and is obtainable with certainty, then the utility of the payoff is the same as the utility of the lottery, i.e. $U(X_{ij}) = U$. Assuming, for example, that $X_1 < X_{ij} < X_2$, the decision maker will obviously prefer X_{ij} to the lottery when $p = 1$ and the lottery to X_{ij} when $p = 0$. Thus, provided utility changes continuously, there will be some intermediate value of p which will make him indifferent between the lottery and the payoff X_{ij}. This value of p can be used to evaluate the utility of X_{ij} using result (2.1). Utilities of other payoffs can be determined in similar fashion provided they all lie between X_1 and X_2. Thus, it is convenient to make X_1 equal to the minimum payoff and X_2 to the maximum, because given their utilities it is possible to establish utilities of all the outcomes in the payoff matrix. The only remaining task is to establish the utilities of X_1 and X_2. Fortunately, this may be done in an arbitrary manner, because the utilities of payoffs obtained in this way do not change their relative position when $U(X_1)$ and $U(X_2)$ (the reference utilities) change. It is convenient to set $U(X_1) = 0$ and $U(X_2) = 1$, where X_1 is the minimum outcome in the payoff matrix and X_2 is the maximum, but any other two numbers will do as well. In this case, when the decision maker is indifferent between payoff X_{ij} and the standard lottery, $U(X_{ij}) = 1 - p$ where p is the value selected by the decision maker.

Having determined utilities of all the payoffs in the manner indicated above, the utility of a strategy in the von Neumann-Morgenstern theory can be readily determined because it is equal to the expected value of the utilities of the individual payoffs. The utility of the ith strategy, for example is given by

$$U(S_i) = \sum_{j=1}^{n} P_j \; U(X_{ij})$$
(2.2)

where P_j is the probability of occurrence of the jth state of nature and X_{ij} is the jth payoff of the ith strategy. The strategy with the highest utility is then selected. For a more detailed exposition of utility theory, see von Neumann and Morgenstern (1947); Luce and Raiffa (1957); Fishburn (1964); Pratt et al (1965); De Groot (1970); Baumol (1972); Whitmore and Findlay (1978); or Hey (1979).

It is worth noting that the standard lottery technique of converting payoffs into utilities takes some account of the decision maker's attitude to risk taking. If he is cautious, he will be indifferent between the standard gamble and a given payoff offered with certainty when p, the weight attached to the utility of the smaller payoff in the standard gamble is small. On the other hand, if he is adventurous, he will be indifferent when p is high for he will not mind the fact that the weight attached to the utility of the smaller payoff is high. This property of the von Neumann-Morgenstern utility theory enhances considerably its attractiveness and has contributed to its wide popularity.

The theory has not gone unchallenged, however. Some critics point out that it is unlikely that the decision maker can be so consistent with his preferences as the theory supposes. He may convert all the payoffs into their subjective utilities using the standard gamble technique, but may then find that the resulting utilities of certain strategies do not agree with his assessment. This may be because he is unwilling to accept the consequences of some axioms which he originally regarded as reasonable, or because there are other aspects of the valuations of payoffs which the utility theory does not take into account. To some extent the problem is similar to the difficulty of establishing decision maker's subjective probabilities of the states of nature (see section 2.6).

One reason the decision maker is often unwilling to accept the resulting utilities of strategies is that no account is taken of the variability of utilities. Two strategies with the same expected utilities are assumed to have the same utility even if their variances differ considerably. Defenders of the theory reply that variability is taken into account when payoffs are converted into utilities. This does not seem to be the case, however, for utilities of individual payoffs of a strategy are determined only in relation to the extreme outcomes in the payoff matrix and not in relation to the other payoffs of the strategy. Allais (1955) was worried by this aspect of the von Neumann-Morgenstern utility theory, but he was also unwilling to accept some of the axioms of the theory.

Finally we may note that some decision analysts prefer to measure utility of a strategy in a different way. They assume that it is a function of the expected payoff of a strategy and its variance (or standard deviation). Its simplest form is a weighted average of the two quantities, the weight being determined subjectively by the decision maker. An approach similar to this is often employed in portfolio analysis (see Markowitz, 1959). Further reference to utility theory and in particular the means and variances of strategies will be made in chapter 5.

3 Decision making based on extreme expected values

3.1 INTRODUCTION

In the previous chapter a description of classical decision theory was given and, in particular, the distinction was made between decision making under risk and decision making under uncertainty. It was also explained that some decision making models have been developed, using a criterion of expected value maximisation, on the basis that precise subjective a priori estimates of the probabilities of future states of nature can be obtained. In many practical decision making problems, it is impossible to obtain objective estimates of the probabilities of future states of nature. However, the techniques, such as those suggested by Savage, for inferring subjective probabilities can be time-consuming and can, on occasions, serve only to demonstrate inconsistency in the face of previous real or hypothetical problems. It is necessary, therefore, to look for an alternative. This must require something less than a precise estimation of probabilities of states of nature, but, on the other hand, must lend itself to the derivation of more valuable insights than are afforded by the use of the classical models of decision making under uncertainty.

One of the first to think in these terms was Fishburn (1964). He assumed that the decision maker possessed enough understanding of the environment of his problem to be able to rank the probabilities of the future states of nature in which his alternative strategies would have to operate. That is, he would be able to state for the n states of nature which he recognised that $P_1 \geqslant P_2 \geqslant \ldots \geqslant P_n$. This is a reasonable compromise between the extremes of risk and uncertainty. It requires neither the very strong assumptions underlying the specification of precise probabilities, nor the implication of decision making under uncertainty that, despite having the knowledge required to estimate an m x n matrix of payoffs, no judgement whatsoever can be formed about the relative likelihood of different states of nature.

In the first main section of this chapter, Fishburn's analysis is described and it is shown how the statistical dominance result which he derived requires assumptions so restrictive as to render the method of little practical value. Section 3.3 shows that Fishburn's result can, in fact, be proved much more directly by using a pair of simple algebraic transformations. Moreover, in section 3.4 by employing the same transformations in conjunction with elementary linear programming concepts, a technique is derived for determining the minimum and maximum expected values for any strategy where the states of nature in which the strategy may have to operate can be ranked in the way proposed by Fishburn. Section 3.5 extends the extreme expected value approach to incorporate strict as well as weak rankings of states of nature. In section 3.6, it is argued that strategy selection in terms of minimum and maximum expected values is a significant addition to the range of formal aids to decision making. By recognising the high probability of the occurrence of incomplete knowledge, such as might be summarised by a ranking of probabilities, rather than pure risk or pure uncertainty, and by developing a technique which uses all the information which is available about the probabilities of states of nature, a decision making aid of real potential value has been devised. Finally, a numerical example is given to demonstrate how strategy choice based on the extreme expected value approach is preferable to the approaches previously available.

3.2 FISHBURN'S STATISTICAL DOMINANCE RESULT

Fishburn considers two strategies, S_1 and S_2. Each strategy may have to operate in one of $j = 1....n$ states of nature and a subjective a priori ranking of the probabilities of the states of nature exists, $P_1 \geqslant P_2 \geqslant ...P_j \geqslant ... \geqslant P_n$. He then seeks to determine under what circumstances the expected value of strategy 1 will exceed or equal that of strategy 2, i.e. $E(S_1) \geqslant E(S_2)$, so that the first strategy could be said to dominate statistically the second.

Fishburn determines the conditions for statistical dominance indirectly, by exploiting Abel's summation identity, see Fishburn (1964), p. 46. The development of his argument is as follows:

Theorem 3.1: If $P_1 \geqslant P_2 \geqslant ... \geqslant P_n$, then $E(S_1) \geqslant E(S_2)$ if $\sum_{k=1}^{j} X_{1k} \geqslant \sum_{k=1}^{j} X_{2k}$

for all $j = 1....n$.
To prove this theorem, Fishburn requires Abel's summation identity as a lemma.

Lemma: $\sum_{j=1}^{n} a_j b_j = \sum_{k=1}^{n-1} (\sum_{j=1}^{k} a_j)(b_k - b_{k+1}) + b_n \sum_{j=1}^{n} a_j$ (3.1)

where $(a_1, a_2, ..., a_n)$ and $(b_1, b_2, ..., b_n)$ are two arbitrary vectors of real numbers.

Proof: Proof follows by straightforward algebraic expansion and simplification of equation (3.1).

A proof of Fishburn's theorem on statistical dominance is now possible:

Proof: $E(S_1) - E(S_2) = \sum_{j=1}^{n} P_j X_{1j} - \sum_{j=1}^{n} P_j X_{2j}$

$$= \sum_{j=1}^{n} P_j (X_{1j} - X_{2j})$$

$$= \sum_{k=1}^{n-1} (\sum_{j=1}^{k} (X_{1j} - X_{2j})) (P_k - P_{k+1})$$

$$+ P_n \sum_{j=1}^{n} (X_{1j} - X_{2j}) \quad (3.2)$$

(By substituting $a_j = (X_{1j} - X_{2j})$ and $b_j = P_j$ in Abel's summation identity)

In this expression, all terms of the form $(P_k - P_{k+1})$ are non-negative as a result of the ranking of the probabilities of states of nature, and so is P_n, since it is an element of a probability distribution.

14

Furthermore, if

$$X_{11} \geq X_{21}$$

$$X_{11} + X_{12} \geq X_{21} + X_{22} \tag{3.3}$$

$$X_{11} + X_{12} + \ldots + X_{1n} \geq X_{21} + X_{22} + \ldots + X_{2n}$$

then it is clear that each element of the right hand side of equation (3.2) is non-negative.

$$\therefore \quad E(S_1) - E(S_2) \geq 0$$

which completes the proof of Fishburn's theorem.

The proof of this theorem is a useful step towards decision making in a situation of incomplete knowledge about probabilities of states of nature. However, its principal practical drawback is clear. Only on a very small number of occasions are the (X_{ij}) in a decision problem likely to obey the very stringent requirements of Fishburn's theorem. It can easily happen that S_1 performs better than S_2 under the most likely state of nature, i.e. $X_{11} > X_{21}$, and therefore the first inequality of (3.3) is satisfied, but S_2 may be greatly preferable to S_1 under the second most likely state of nature, i.e. $X_{22} > X_{12}$, so that the second inequality is not satisfied. If some practical decision making aid is to be developed, a more general result than this is required, even if it may not be so unambiguous in its interpretation.

3.3 AN ALTERNATIVE PROOF OF FISHBURN'S THEOREM

As the first step in the development of a more practically useful decision making rule, an alternative proof of Fishburn's dominance result may be derived. This does not depend directly on Abel's summation identity.

<u>Proof:</u> $E(S_1) - E(S_2) = \sum_{j=1}^{n} P_j X_{1j} - \sum_{j=1}^{n} P_j X_{2j}$

Let $Q_j = P_j - P_{j+1}$ $(j = 1 \ldots (n-1))$

$Q_n = P_n$ (since, by implication $P_{n+1} = 0$) $\Big\}$ (3.4)

$Y_{ij} = \sum_{k=1}^{j} X_{ik}$ $(i = 1, 2; j = 1 \ldots n)$ \tag{3.5}

Then $\sum_{j=1}^{n} P_j X_{ij} = P_1 X_{i1} + P_2 X_{i2} + \ldots + P_n X_{in}$

$= (Q_1 + Q_2 + \ldots + Q_n) X_{i1} + (Q_2 + Q_3 + \ldots + Q_n) X_{i2}$

$+ \ldots + Q_n X_{in}$

$= \sum_{j=1}^{n} Q_j Y_{ij}$

$$\therefore \quad E(S_1) - E(S_2) = \sum_{j=1}^{n} Q_j Y_{1j} - \sum_{j=1}^{n} Q_j Y_{2j}$$

$$= \sum_{j=1}^{n} Q_j (Y_{1j} - Y_{2j})$$

Because of the ranking constraint on the probabilities of states of nature, all terms Q_j ($= P_j - P_{j+1}$) are non-negative. Therefore, provided all terms $(Y_{1j} - Y_{2j})$ are non-negative, $E(S_1) - E(S_2) \geqslant 0$. But $(Y_{1j} - Y_{2j})$ is merely $(\sum_{k=1}^{j} X_{1k} - \sum_{k=1}^{j} X_{2k})$. It follows, therefore, that if the ranking conditions (3.3) hold, $E(S_1) \geqslant E(S_2)$. Hence the proof is completed.

3.4 THE DERIVATION OF MAXIMUM AND MINIMUM EXPECTED VALUES GIVEN WEAK RANKING OF PROBABILITIES

The second proof of Fishburn's theorem, although a little more direct than the original, is of interest not so much for itself as for the introduction of the two sets of transformations involving Q_j and Y_j. By employing these transformations, Cannon and Kmietowicz (1974) showed that it was possible to derive, by a simple analytical method, expressions for the minimum and maximum expected values of any strategy, where the states of nature in which the strategy might have to operate are again subject to the probability ranking constraint, $P_1 \geqslant P_2 \geqslant \ldots \geqslant P_n$. This type of ranking will be called weak ranking to distinguish it from strict ranking described in section 3.5. It is this derivation which forms the foundation of our approach to decision making in the face of incomplete knowledge.

For simplicity of exposition and notation, suppose that it is desired to determine the extreme expected values, E(S) of a single strategy, S. Under the assumptions already described, this problem may be formalised as the following pair of linear programming problems:

<u>Maximise or Minimise</u> $\quad E(S) = \sum_{j=1}^{n} P_j X_j$

<u>subject to</u>

$$\sum_{j=1}^{n} P_j = 1 \tag{3.6}$$

$$P_j - P_{j+1} \geqslant 0 \ (j = 1 \ldots (n-1)) \tag{3.7}$$

$$P_j \geqslant 0 \qquad (j = 1 \ldots n) \tag{3.8}$$

This linear programming problem may be simplified greatly by the application of the transformations (3.4) and (3.5). As a result of the use of these transformations, the constraints of the linear programming problem collapse into just one functional constraint, (3.9) and n non-negativity constraints, (3.10). The transformed problem is:

<u>Maximise or Minimise</u> $\quad E(S) = \sum_{j=1}^{n} Q_j Y_j$

<u>subject to</u>
$$\sum_{j=1}^{n} jQ_j = 1 \qquad\qquad (3.9)$$

$$Q_j \geq 0 \qquad (j = 1....n) \qquad (3.10)$$

Constraints (3.10) replace (3.7), noting again that $Q_n = P_n$ since P_{n+1} is implicitly zero. Also

$$\sum_{j=1}^{n} jQ_j = Q_1 + 2Q_2 + 3Q_3 + ... + nQ_n$$

$$= (P_1 - P_2) + 2(P_2 - P_3) + 3(P_3 - P_4) + ...nP_n$$

$$= \sum_{j=1}^{n} P_j = 1$$

Hence (3.9) ensures that (3.6) will hold. Finally, $P_j = \sum_{k=j}^{n} Q_k$ for all j, which, since $Q_j \geq 0$, ensures that $P_j \geq 0$ and, therefore, that (3.8) holds. Hence solving the transformed linear programming problem is directly equivalent to solving the original one.

Examination of the transformed problem reveals one very interesting feature. The problem has only one functional constraint and, therefore, by the linear programming theorem of the basis, if a finite optimal solution exists, it will have an optimal solution with only one of the decision variables non-negative, and all other Q_j zero. Further, from (3.9), if only one Q_j is non-zero, it must take the value 1/j. Referring now to the objective function, it is clear that it will be maximised when Y_j/j is maximised and minimised when Y_j/j is minimised. Hence the extreme expected payoffs of any strategy, given an <u>a priori</u> ranking of the probabilities of the states of nature, may be found by computing the n partial averages

$$\frac{1}{j}Y_j = \frac{1}{j} \sum_{k=1}^{j} X_k = \bar{X}_j \qquad\qquad (3.11)$$

for j = 1....n

The largest such partial average will be the maximum expected payoff and the smallest will be the minimum expected payoff.

3.5 THE DERIVATION OF MAXIMUM AND MINIMUM EXPECTED VALUES GIVEN STRICT RANKING OF PROBABILITIES

In the previous section it was assumed that the decision maker was able to state a weak ranking of probabilities of the states of nature, i.e. $P_j - P_{j+1} \geq 0$, for j = 1, 2....n where $P_{n+1} = 0$. If he has some more information and is able to specify a strict ranking of probabilities, i.e. $P_j - P_{j+1} \geq K_j$, j = 1, 2....n where again $P_{n+1} = 0$ and where the K_j are positive constants, it is also possible to find the maximum and minimum expected payoffs for strategies. The strict ranking of probabilities assumes that successive probabilities differ from each other by at least a given amount, e.g. if $K_j = 1/10$, P_j exceeds P_{j+1} by at least 1/10. It is plausible to assume that certain decision makers may be able to specify some, if not all, of the K_j.

In order to find maximum and minimum expected payoffs of a strategy, it is necessary to solve the following linear programming problem:

<u>Maximise or Minimise</u> $E(S) = \sum_{j=1}^{n} P_j X_j$

<u>subject to</u> $\sum_{j=1}^{n} P_j = 1$

$$P_j - P_{j+1} \geq K_j \qquad (j = 1, 2\ldots n; \; P_{n+1} = 0)$$

$$P_j \geq 0 \qquad (j = 1, 2\ldots n) \qquad (3.12)$$

where the P_j are variables and the X_j and K_j known constants. Note that the K_j must be chosen such that $\sum_{j=1}^{n} jK_j < 1$. If $\sum_{j=1}^{n} jK_j > 1$, it can be readily shown that $\sum_{j=1}^{n} P_j > 1$, which is precluded by the first constraint of expression (3.12). If $\sum_{j=1}^{n} jK_j = 1$, the probabilities are uniquely defined, i.e. $P_j = \sum_{k=j}^{n} K_k$, for $j = 1, 2\ldots n$, and so is E(S).

The above pair of linear programming problems may be greatly simplified by employing the following transformations:

$$Y_j = \sum_{k=1}^{j} X_k, \qquad (j = 1, 2\ldots n)$$

which is the same as (3.5), and

$$Q_j' = P_j - P_{j+1} - K_j , (j = 1, 2\ldots n) \qquad (3.13)$$

which is analogous to (3.4).

Using the new variables and algebraic manipulations similar to those employed in section 3.3, it can be shown that the linear programme given in (3.12) may be rewritten as

<u>Maximise or Minimise</u> $E(S) = \sum_{j=1}^{n} Q_j' Y_j + \sum_{j=1}^{n} K_j Y_j$

<u>subject to</u> $\sum_{j=1}^{n} jQ_j' + \sum_{j=1}^{n} jK_j = 1$

$$Q_j' \geq 0 \qquad (j = 1, 2\ldots n) \qquad (3.14)$$

Note that the second substantive constraint and the $P_j \geq 0$ constraint of (3.12) have been compressed into a single, $Q_j' \geq 0$ constraint. The problem as specified in (3.14) has one functional constraint, and, therefore, by the linear programming theorem of the basis, if a finite optimum solution exists, it will occur when one of the decision variables is non-zero and all the others are equal to zero. From the substantive constraint of (3.14), it follows that the value of the decision variable is given by

$$Q_j' = \frac{1}{j} (1 - \sum_{j=1}^{n} jK_j) \qquad (3.15)$$

Inserting this value in the objective function of (3.14), we get

$$E(S) = \frac{1}{j}Y_j \; (1 - \sum_{j=1}^{n} jK_j) + \sum_{j=1}^{n} K_j Y_j \qquad (3.16)$$

Thus, as in section 3.3, the optimum values of E(S) may be found by evaluating (3.16) for j = 1, 2....n. The largest of these gives the maximum E(S) and the smallest the minimum.

Note that when $K_j = 0$, for j = 1, 2....n, (3.16) reduces to

$$E(S) = \frac{1}{j}Y_j = \frac{1}{j} \sum_{k=1}^{j} X_k = \bar{X}_j \qquad (3.17)$$

which is the same as (3.11) obtained above. This shows that the results for optimum E(S) obtained under conditions of weak ranking of probabilities of the states of nature are special cases of the more general results involving strict ranking of probabilities.

Note also that the value of j which optimises (3.16) is the same as that which optimises (3.17). This is so because the part of (3.16) which varies with j is the same as (3.17). Thus if optimum E(S) for the case of weak ranking is calculated first, optimum E(S) for the case of strict ranking may be obtained immediately by evaluating (3.16) for the optimum value of j found earlier. It follows from (3.16) and (3.17) that

$$\left.\begin{array}{c}\text{maximum}\\ \text{minimum}\end{array}\right\}E(S)_{s.r.} = \left.\begin{array}{c}\text{maximum}\\ \text{minimum}\end{array}\right\}E(S)_{w.r.} \; (1 - \sum_{j=1}^{n} jK_j) + \sum_{j=1}^{n} K_j Y_j \quad (3.18)$$

where s.r. = strict ranking and w.r. = weak ranking. Expression (3.18) may be used to calculate maximum and minimum $E(S)_{s.r.}$ when maximum and minimum $E(S)_{w.r.}$ are available.

It is also possible to establish a relationship between max $E(S)_{w.r.}$ and max $E(S)_{s.r.}$, and min $E(S)_{w.r.}$ and min $E(S)_{s.r.}$. Strict ranking limits the range of probabilities of states of nature more than weak ranking and thus eliminates some probability distributions which weak ranking does not. One could expect, therefore, that max $E(S)_{w.r.} \geqslant$ max $E(S)_{s.r.}$ To prove this assertion consider the difference

$$\text{max } E(S)_{w.r.} - \text{max } E(S)_{s.r.}$$

Suppose j* is the value of j which gives max E(S) for both types of ranking. Then from (3.16) and (3.17) the difference may be rewritten as:

$$\frac{1}{j*} Y_{j*} - \frac{1}{j*} Y_{j*} \; (1 - \sum_{j=1}^{n} jK_j) - \sum_{j=1}^{n} K_j Y_j$$

$$= \bar{X}_{j*} - \bar{X}_{j*} \; (1 - \sum_{j=1}^{n} jK_j) - \sum_{j=1}^{n} K_j Y_j$$

$$= \bar{X}_{j*} \sum_{j=1}^{n} jK_j - \sum_{j=1}^{n} K_j Y_j$$

$$= \bar{X}_{j*} \sum_{j=1}^{n} jK_j - \sum_{j=1}^{n} K_j \, j\bar{X}_j \qquad \text{(since } Y_j = j\bar{X}_j)$$

$$= \sum_{j=1}^{n} jK_j \; (\bar{X}_{j*} - \bar{X}_j) \qquad \text{which is}$$

$\geqslant 0$ by definition since $\bar{X}_{j*}$ is the largest partial average of the payoffs.

A similar procedure may be used to show that

$$\min E(S)_{w.r.} \leq \min E(S)_{s.r.}$$

It is also of interest to identify the probability distribution which produces optimum E(S) in the case of strict ranking of probabilities. This may be done simply by rewriting (3.16) in terms of the X_j rather than the Y_j and identifying the coefficients of each X_j which, by definition of E(S), are equal to the corresponding probabilities, P_j. A different procedure is followed below because it gives an insight into the mechanics of the process which locates the optimal expected values.

It was mentioned previously that the optimum value of E(S) would occur when one decision variable was non-zero and the rest all zero. If j^* is the value of j which optimises (3.16), so that $Q'_{j^*} \neq 0$, then the value of Q'_{j^*} determined by (3.15) can be regarded as the maximum value attainable as Q'_{j^*} is increased from zero, i.e. treating (3.15) temporarily as an inequality rather than as an equation constraint. Maximising Q'_{j^*} implies maximising

$$Q'_{j^*} = P_{j^*} - P_{j^*+1} - K_{j^*} = \frac{1}{j^*} (1 - \sum_{j=1}^{n} jK_j) \qquad (3.19)$$

which will occur when P_{j^*} is as large as possible and P_{j^*+1} as small as possible (K_{j^*} is a constant). The smallest value of P_{j^*+1} consistent with strict ranking arises when $P_n = K_n$, $P_{n-1} = K_{n-1} + K_n$, etc. and, therefore, in general

$$P_j = \sum_{r=j}^{n} K_r \quad \text{for } j = j^*+1, \ldots n \qquad (3.20)$$

Substituting for P_{j^*+1} from (3.20) into (3.19) and rearranging, we have

$$P_{j^*} = \frac{1}{j^*} (1 - \sum_{j=1}^{n} jK_j) + \sum_{j=j^*}^{n} K_j \qquad (3.21)$$

Now if P_{j^*} is made as large as possible, then $P_1, P_2 \ldots P_{j^*-1}$ must be as small as possible, but must still satisfy the strict ranking constraint, i.e.

$$P_{j^*-1} = P_{j^*} + K_{j^*-1}$$

$$P_{j^*-2} = P_{j^*} + K_{j^*-1} + K_{j^*-2}$$

$$\begin{array}{ccc} \cdot & \cdot & \cdot \\ \cdot & \cdot & \cdot \\ \cdot & \cdot & \cdot \end{array}$$

$$P_1 = P_{j^*} + \sum_{j=1}^{j^*-1} K_j \qquad (3.22)$$

Substituting for P_{j^*} from (3.21) into (3.22) and generalising, we have,

$$P_j = \frac{1}{j^*} (1 - \sum_{j=1}^{n} jK_j) + \sum_{r=j}^{n} K_r, \qquad j = 1, 2 \ldots j^* \qquad (3.23)$$

Thus (3.20) and (3.23) specify all the probabilities at the optimum and it can be readily checked that their sum is equal to one, i.e.

$$\sum_{j=1}^{n} P_j = \sum_{j=1}^{j^*} \left(\frac{1}{j^*}(1 - \sum_{j=1}^{n} jK_j) + \sum_{r=j}^{n} K_r\right) + \sum_{j=j^*+1}^{n} \sum_{r=j}^{n} K_r$$

$$= (1 - \sum_{j=r}^{n} jK_j) + \sum_{j=1}^{n} \sum_{r=j}^{n} K_r$$

$$= 1 - \sum_{j=1}^{n} jK_j + \sum_{j=1}^{n} jK_j = 1 \quad \text{as required.}$$

Results (3.20) and (3.23) confirm that if $K_j > 0$, for $j = 1, 2 \ldots n$, then $P_j > 0$ for $j = 1, 2 \ldots n$. When $j^* = n$, then $P_n = 1 - \sum_{j=1}^{n-1} K_j$.

It is also worth noting that in the case of weak ranking of probabilities, the probability distribution applicable at the optimum arose in a similar manner. The maximum value of $P_{j^*} - P_{j^*+1}$ was obtained by making P_{j^*+1} as small as possible within the ranking constraint, i.e. zero, and P_{j^*} as large as possible, i.e. $\frac{1}{j^*}$.

3.6 THE SIGNIFICANCE AND USE OF MAXIMUM AND MINIMUM EXPECTED VALUES

In chapter 2, it was argued that both the theoretical extremes of decision making under risk and decision making under uncertainty were unrealistic in their assumptions concerning what was known about the probabilities of the states of nature. To assume known probabilities was overestimating the understanding the decision maker would be likely to have of his problem environment. To use complete ignorance methods and to imply thereby no understanding of the relative probabilities of states of nature would be an underestimate. This is because in many realistic situations decision makers can utilise their past experience and their awareness of current developments to form some opinion for themselves about probabilities. It is quite likely, for example, that an industrialist considering expansion of productive capacity will have a view as to the relative probabilities of the timing of an expected upturn in world trade and thus of the likely profitability of different investment strategies. Identification, therefore, of an a priori ordinal ranking of states of nature is a much closer approximation to reality. If the decision maker can produce a strict ranking of probabilities of states of nature, so much the better. Furthermore, given this ranking, any decision making criterion which ignores it is likely to be inferior to one which takes it into account. This is because the calculation of maximum and minimum expected payoffs takes the fullest possible account of the circumstances in which the different strategies may have to operate.

Consider first the cautious decision maker, using the maximin criterion. The superiority of the extreme expected value approach over the complete ignorance equivalent is assured, provided that the outcomes of decisions may be averaged and on the assumption that a malevolent nature will, within the bounds stated, always adjust the actual probabilities of states of nature in the way least favourable to the decision maker. He can be sure that he will achieve better results over a large number of decisions by using maximin expected payoff rather than pure maximin payoff. This is so because the strategy which has the maximin expected payoff can never have a lower minimum expected payoff than does a different strategy which has the maximin payoff. Of course, the strategy which actually has the maximum expected payoff cannot, in general, be identified either by complete ignorance methods or by the extreme expected value approach. The strategy selected by the latter method need not, therefore, always correspond to the best strategy which could have been selected by a decision maker with firm knowledge of the probabilities of states of nature. Given the information available, however, and the expectation about the perverse behaviour of nature, a strategy chosen on the basis of extreme expected value must be the best for the decision maker concerned.

Similarly, a decision maker who is willing to take great risks can be confident that he will achieve better results over a large number of decisions by using maximax expected payoff rather than pure maximax payoff, assuming now a benevolent nature. This is because a strategy which has the highest maximum expected payoff can have no lower maximum expected payoff than does a different strategy which has the maximax payoff. If the maximax decision maker believes that nature will ensure that, within the region of his ignorance, events are favourable to his choice, he can expect to fare better by using the maximax expected payoff criterion rather than by adopting pure maximax.

A similar argument can be developed for applying the Hurwicz criterion to extreme expected payoffs rather than to extreme payoffs. This is true also of a decision maker who relies upon the minimax regret criterion. He can expect less regret if he relies on minimax expected regret rather than on minimax regret. Thus, in general, when maximum and minimum expected payoffs rather than pure limiting payoffs are used for decision making, full use is made of available information and intermediate payoffs are taken into account. Also, the region of ignorance is defined as closely as possible and probabilities of states of nature are distinguished from attitudes towards chance and regret and from attitudes towards the unknown.

Decision making in terms of extreme expected values is likely to be at its most superior to the corresponding complete ignorance decision rules under the following circumstances:

  (i)   When a number of decisions are taken in different conditions, that is, when strategies, states of nature, payoffs and ranking change from one decision problem to another. The expected value concept will be appropriate if it is possible to average the outcomes of several decisions. Such conditions could well apply to many managerial decisions.

  (ii)   When the number of states of nature is large. In this situation, reliance on maximum and minimum expected payoffs is undesirable as it ignores a large number of intermediate payoffs.

  (iii) When the same problem is faced by the decision maker a small number of times (up to ten or so). The expected value approach is again appropriate in this case if the results of decision making can be averaged over the outcomes. If the decision is taken a large number of times under identical conditions, however, a point will soon be reached when it will be possible to make fairly reliable empirical estimates of the probabilities

of the states of nature, which can then be used in a
conventional expected value calculation. A sequential approach
to this problem will be discussed in chapter 7.

The expected value approach developed in this chapter is most suitable
when conditions (i) or (ii) and (iii) are fulfilled simultaneously.
When an isolated and important decision is taken, the expected value
approach alone is less suitable, but it may still be of help when there
are many states of nature. Here, the minimum payoffs of strategies, as
used by the pure maximin criterion, may also be relevant.

3.7   A NUMERICAL EXAMPLE

In this section a numerical example is presented to illustrate the
methods developed in sections 3.2, 3.4 and 3.5. Suppose a businessman
is faced with the choice between two investment projects, A and B,
involving the same outlay. His financial resources are limited and,
therefore, he must choose either A or B, but not both. Project A
involves an investment in manufacturing and thus its profitability
depends on the growth of demand in the sector, while B is an investment
in financial securities so its profitability depends on the level of
interest rates. Suppose four possible states of nature are identified
and are numbered in decreasing order of probability of occurrence:
(1)growth of demand for manufactures and an unchanged level of interest
rates; (2)unchanged demand for manufactures and a high level of rates of
interest; (3)rapid growth in demand for manufactures and negative real
rates of interest; (4)demand for manufactures higher than at present and
extremely high rates of interest. Assume first that only a weak ranking
of probabilities of the states of nature is possible, i.e. $P_1 \geqslant P_2 \geqslant P_3 \geqslant P_4$. The estimated payoff matrix is shown in Figure 3.1.

	State of Nature			
Strategy	1	2	3	4
A	$7\frac{1}{2}$	-5	15	9
B	$5\frac{1}{2}$	9	-5	15

Figure 3.1   Payoff Matrix for the Numerical Example

The entries in the body of Figure 3.1 correspond to returns on capital
invested, e.g. if project A is adopted and state of nature 1 occurs, the
expected return on capital is $7\frac{1}{2}$ per cent.

An inspection of Figure 3.1 confirms that neither strategy dominates
the other in the sense discussed in section 3.2. Referring to (3.3) we
note that $7\frac{1}{2} > 5\frac{1}{2}$ but $(7\frac{1}{2} - 5) < (5\frac{1}{2} + 9)$ and therefore neither strategy
dominates the other. Moreover, the minimum and maximum payoffs of the
two strategies are the same so that the maximin, maximax and Hurwicz
criteria cannot distinguish between them. The minimax regret criterion
favours A, as does the Bayes-Laplace criterion.

So far no account has been taken of the fact that the probabilities of
the states of nature have been ranked. The results developed in section
3.4 can be used to calculate the maximum and minimum expected payoffs
for each strategy. Using result (3.11) we calculate partial averages

23

for the two strategies as:

Strategy A		
$\bar{X}_1 = (1/1)(7\frac{1}{2})$	$= 7\frac{1}{2}$
$\bar{X}_2 = (\frac{1}{2})(7\frac{1}{2} - 5)$	$= 1\frac{1}{4}$
$\bar{X}_3 = (1/3)(7\frac{1}{2} - 5 + 15)$	$= 5^5/_6$
$\bar{X}_4 = (\frac{1}{4})(7\frac{1}{2} - 5 + 15 + 9)$	$= 6^5/_8$

Strategy B		
$\bar{X}_1 = (1/1)(5\frac{1}{2})$	$= 5\frac{1}{2}$
$\bar{X}_2 = (\frac{1}{2})(5\frac{1}{2} + 9)$	$= 7\frac{1}{4}$
$\bar{X}_3 = (1/3)(5\frac{1}{2} + 9 - 5)$	$= 3^1/_6$
$\bar{X}_4 = (\frac{1}{4})(5\frac{1}{2} + 9 - 5 + 15)$	$= 6^1/_8$

For each strategy, the largest partial average gives the maximum expected payoff and the smallest the minimum, i.e. for A the maximum is $7\frac{1}{2}$ and the minimum $1\frac{1}{4}$ and for B the maximum is $7\frac{1}{4}$ and the minimum $3^1/_6$.

The most striking feature of the above results is the marked change in the attractiveness of strategy B revealed by the use of ranked probabilities in the calculation of extreme expected values. The maximin expected payoff criterion clearly selects B, as $3^1/_6 > 1\frac{1}{4}$, while there is only a marginal preference for A when the maximax expected payoff criterion is used, as $7\frac{1}{2}$ is only slightly larger than $7\frac{1}{4}$. Moreover, the Hurwicz criterion applied to the extreme expected values will also favour B, except in cases of extreme optimism. The minimax expected regret criterion still favours A, but only by a small margin (7 as against $7^1/_3$).[1] The expected value approach recognises the important advantage B has over A under the second most likely state of nature. A is much preferable to B under the third state of nature, but because of its low ranking, the advantage is less important.

Finally, it is again possible to calculate extreme expected payoffs for each strategy, if the decision maker is able to specify a strict rather than a weak ranking of probabilities of states of nature. Suppose the decision maker has the following a priori beliefs about the ranking of probabilities of states of nature: $P_1 - P_2 \geq 0$; $P_2 - P_3 \geq \frac{1}{4}$; $P_3 - P_4 \geq 1/8$; and $P_4 - P_5 \geq 0$, where $P_5 = 0$ by definition. In terms of the algebra of section 3.5, $K_1 = 0$, $K_2 = \frac{1}{4}$, $K_3 = 1/8$ and $K_4 = 0$. For example, now the decision maker believes that P_2 exceeds P_3 by at least $\frac{1}{4}$, while in the case of weak ranking he was only able to say that P_2 was larger than or equal to P_3.

Given the information mentioned above, it is possible to calculate extreme expected payoffs for strategies using result (3.16), i.e. evaluating the result for j = 1, 2, 3, 4; the largest of these values gives the maximum expected payoff and the smallest the minimum. A quicker method of finding these values is to use the relationship between results (3.11) or (3.17) and (3.16) discussed in section 3.5. This shows that maximum expected value for the case of weak and strict ranking of probabilities occurs for the same value of j. The same applies to minimum expected value. Moreover, the maxima and minima are related by result (3.18). Using these relationships, we first note that for strategy A maximum expected payoff for the case of weak ranking occurs when j = 1, and then E(S) = $7\frac{1}{2}$; and, therefore, using result (3.18),

$$\max E(S)_{s.r.} = 7\frac{1}{2} (1 - 7/_8) + 45/16 = 3\frac{3}{4}$$

where

$$\sum_{j=1}^{4} jK_j = 1(0) + 2(\tfrac{1}{4}) + 3(1/_8) + 4(0) = 7/_8 \text{ and}$$

$$\sum_{j=1}^{4} K_j Y_j = \sum_{j=1}^{4} K_j \sum_{r=1}^{j} X_r = 0(7\tfrac{1}{2}) + \tfrac{1}{4}(7\tfrac{1}{2} - 5) + 1/_8(7\tfrac{1}{2} + 5 + 15)$$

$$+ 0(7\tfrac{1}{2} - 5 + 15 + 9) = \frac{45}{16}$$

Minimum expected payoff for strategy A for the case of weak ranking of probabilities occurs when $j = 2$ and equals $1\tfrac{1}{4}$ and therefore using result (3.18) again

$$\min E(S)_{s.r.} = 1\tfrac{1}{4}(1 - 7/_8) + \frac{45}{16} = 2\frac{31}{32}.$$

Using a similar procedure for strategy B, it can be readily found that

$$\max E(S)_{s.r.} = 5\frac{23}{32} \text{ and } \min E(S)_{s.r.} = 5\frac{5}{24}.$$

Examining the results obtained for the case of strict ranking, we see that now strategy B is even more attractive than strategy A. Its minimum expected value is $5^5/_{24}$ while for strategy A it is only $2^{31}/_{32}$. Moreover, now maximum expected payoff is $5^{23}/_{32}$ for strategy B, but only $3\tfrac{3}{4}$ for strategy A. Thus, both maximin and maximax criteria now favour strategy B.

It is also worth noting that for both strategies the range of expected payoff is much smaller in the case of strict ranking than in the case of weak ranking. For strategy A the ranges are: $3\tfrac{3}{4} - 2^{31}/_{32} = 25/_{32}$ and $7\tfrac{1}{2} - 1\tfrac{1}{4} = 6\tfrac{1}{4}$ respectively; and for strategy B they are: $5^{23}/_{32} - 5^5/_{24} = 31/_{64}$ and $7\tfrac{1}{4} - 31/_6 = 41/_{12}$ respectively. These results confirm the general relationship between maximum and minimum expected payoffs specified in expressions (3.19) and (3.20). The range of expected payoff for the case of strict ranking is always smaller than or equal to the range for the case of weak ranking because the additional constraints imposed by strict ranking of probabilities eliminate many probability distributions which weak ranking allows. As the results of the above example suggest, the reduction in the range of expected payoff due to the introduction of strict ranking can be very great.

Note finally that in spite of the fact that the value of j which yields maximum expected payoff for the case of weak and strict ranking of probabilities is the same, the probability distributions applicable at the maximum are different. For example, considering strategy A, in the case of weak ranking the probability distribution is $P_1 = 1$, $P_2 = P_3 = P_4 = 0$, while in the case of strict ranking the distribution is given by results (3.20) and (3.23): $P_1 = 1/_1 (1 - (7/_8)) + (0 + \tfrac{1}{4} + 1/_8 + 0) = \tfrac{1}{2}$; $P_2 = \tfrac{1}{4} + 1/_8 + 0 = 3/_8$; $P_3 = 1/_8 + 0 = 1/_8$; $P_4 = 0$. As required, $P_1 + P_2 + P_3 + P_4 = 1$. In both cases the optimum value of j is one.

The probability distribution yielding the minimum expected payoff in the case of weak ranking arises when $j = 2$ and is given by: $P_1 = P_2 = \tfrac{1}{2}$, $P_3 = P_4 = 0$. In the case of strict ranking, the probability distribution is again given by results (3.20) and (3.23):

$P_1 = (\frac{1}{2})(1 - 7/8) + (0 + \frac{1}{4} + 1/8 + 0) = 7/16$, $P_2 = (\frac{1}{2})(1 - 7/8) + (\frac{1}{4} + 1/8 + 0) = 7/16$, $P_3 = 1/8 + 0 = 1/8$, $P_4 = 0$. Again, $P_1+P_2+P_3+P_4 = 1$ as required.

It can be readily confirmed that if these probability distributions are used to calculate expected payoffs for strategy A, they yield $3\frac{3}{4}$ and $2^{31}/_{32}$, which are respectively the maximum and minimum obtained above.

NOTES

(1) The regret matrix corresponding to the payoff matrix shown in Figure 3.1 is given by

	State of Nature			
Strategy	1	2	3	4
A	0	14	0	6
B	2	0	20	0

Partial averages of the regrets for strategy A are: $\bar{R}_1 = 0$, $\bar{R}_2 = 7$, $\bar{R}_3 = 4 2/3$, $\bar{R}_4 = 5$, and for strategy B: $\bar{R}_1 = 2$, $\bar{R}_2 = 1$, $\bar{R}_3 = 7 1/3$, $\bar{R}_4 = 5$. Therefore, the maximum expected regret for strategy A is 7 and for B, $71/3$.

4 The role of maximum variance in strategy choice

4.1 INTRODUCTION

As a result of the technique developed in section 3.4, it is now possible
to compare strategies on the basis of their minimum or maximum expected
values, their maximum expected regret, or any appropriate combination of
the three. This alone represents a considerable step forward from the
pure risk and pure uncertainty models outlined in Chapter 2. However,
the remaining uncertainty about which state of nature will occur, even
within the ranking constraint, implies the existence of another
consideration which the decision maker might well wish to bear in mind
in choosing between strategies. This is the dispersion of the potential
payoffs. The decision maker's attitude to risk may be such that he would
be prepared to turn down a strategy with a higher expected value in
favour of one which offered a lower mean payoff, but with a higher
probability of an actual outcome close to that expectation. (1)
Diagrammatically, it may be that strategy A will be preferred to strategy
B (see Figure 4.1).

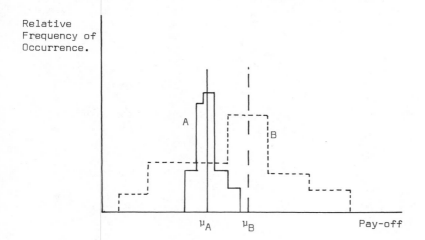

Figure 4.1   Comparison of Strategies on the basis of both Mean Value and
              Dispersion

In this chapter, it is shown that, by using variance (or standard deviation) as an index of dispersion, maximum and minimum values of the index, consistent with an a priori ranking of the states of nature, may be found. Section 4.1 shows how the extreme variance problem may be formulated as a quadratic programme of a special kind. Section 4.2 discusses the solution of this problem when there are only two states of nature. Section 4.3 demonstrates the solution for more than two states of nature. As with the extreme expected values, it is found that the extreme variances can, in fact, be calculated using nothing more than straightforward arithmetic. A numerical example is given in the final section.

4.2 THE EXTREME VARIANCES OF PAYOFFS

If dispersion is of interest in strategy choice, it follows that any statement which can be made about the variance of payoff of a strategy has potential value. However, just as incomplete knowledge about the probability distribution of states of nature proscribed any possibility of making a precise statement about expected payoff, so it does about the variance of payoffs. Nevertheless, some valuable information may be derived, in particular by examining the maximum variance of payoffs, given the previously adopted assumption of states of nature ranked in terms of probability.

If the concern is now with variance extrema, a new pair of optimisation problems must be considered where, again assuming a single strategy for the sake of simplicity, the objective function is:

$$\text{Var (S)} = \sum_{j=1}^{n} P_j (X_j - \bar{X})^2$$

$$= \sum_{j=1}^{n} P_j X_j^2 - \left(\sum_{j=1}^{n} P_j X_j \right)^2$$

The constraints on this optimisation are as in the extreme expected value problem:

$$\sum_{j=1}^{n} P_j = 1 \qquad\qquad (4.1)$$

$$P_j - P_{j+1} \geq 0 \quad (j = 1 \ldots (n-1)) \qquad (4.2)$$

$$P_j \geq 0 \quad (j = 1 \ldots \ldots n) \qquad (4.3)$$

As before, the crucial step in developing a general result is the application of a series of transformations:

$$Q_j = P_j - P_{j+1} (j = 1 \ldots (n-1))$$

$$Y_j = \sum_{k=1}^{j} X_k \quad (j = 1 \ldots \ldots n)$$

$$Z_j = \sum_{k=1}^{j} X_k^2 \quad (j = 1 \ldots \ldots n)$$

On the basis of essentially the same argument as was advanced in section 3.4, the original pair of optimisation problems may be re-expressed as:

$$\underline{\text{Maximise or Minimise }} \text{Var (S)} = \sum_{j=1}^{n} Z_j Q_j - \left(\sum_{j=1}^{n} Y_j Q_j \right)^2$$

$$\underline{\text{Subject to}} \qquad \sum_{j=1}^{n} j Q_j = 1 \qquad\qquad\qquad (4.4)$$

$$Q_j \geq 0 \qquad (j = 1 \ldots n) \qquad (4.5)$$

If the objective function of the transformed problem is now examined, it is readily apparent that it is a quadratic function of the Q_j. Furthermore, it is easily re-written in the form

$$\text{Var (S)} = \sum_{j=1}^{n} Z_j Q_j - \tfrac{1}{2} \sum_{j=1}^{n} \sum_{h=1}^{n} Y^*_{jh} Q_j Q_h$$

where the term $\sum_{j=1}^{n} \sum_{h=1}^{n} Y^*_{jh} Q_j Q_h$ is non-negative and where the Y^*_{jh}

are such that $Y^*_{jh} = Y^*_{hj}$. This is because it derives from the square $\left(\sum_{j=1}^{n} Y_j Q_j \right)^2$, i.e. $Y^*_{jh} = 2 Y_j Y_h$. However, this condition is sufficient to

ensure that the objective function is concave to the origin, see, for example, Hillier and Lieberman (1974), pp. 725/6. Thus the problem is a standard quadratic programming problem of optimising a (concave) quadratic objective function subject to linear constraints. But in this case there is just one constraint and this is an equality constraint. Hence it transpires that a solution to the problem may be found in a semi-analytical fashion and much more easily than in the general quadratic programming case.

4.3 SOLUTION OF THE PROBLEM IN TWO DIMENSIONS

Consider a simple two dimensional example.

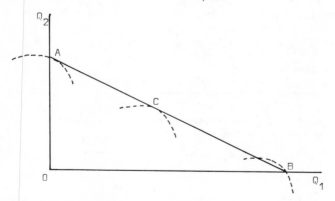

Figure 4.2   The Two-dimensional Extreme Variance Problem

Since the optimum $(Q_1 Q_2)$ combination must lie on the constraint line, but within the positive quadrant, the only positions at which it is possible for an optimum to lie are:

(a) At the intersection of the constraint line with one of the two axes, as in A or B;

(b) At a tangency point, such as C.

However, it may be shown that points of type C cannot occur in the two-dimensional version of this particular problem. To demonstrate this, ignore temporarily the non-negativity constraints on the Q_j and use the standard Lagrange multiplier approach to endeavour to identify the values of Q_j which optimise the objective function, subject only to the single constraint,

$$\sum_{j=1}^{2} j Q_j = 1.$$

The appropriate Lagrangian is

$$L = Z_1 Q_1 + Z_2 Q_2 - (Y_1 Q_1 + Y_2 Q_2)^2 + \lambda (1 - Q_1 - 2Q_2)$$

For an optimum, it is necessary that the three simultaneous equations formed from the partial derivatives of L with respect to Q_1, Q_2 and λ be soluble for Q_1, Q_2 and λ. That is, it must be possible to solve:

$$\frac{\partial L}{\partial Q_1} = Z_1 - 2Y_1^2 Q_1 - 2Y_1 Y_2 Q_2 - \lambda = 0 \qquad (4.6)$$

$$\frac{\partial L}{\partial Q_2} = Z_2 - 2Y_1 Y_2 Q_1 - 2Y_2^2 Q_2 - 2\lambda = 0 \qquad (4.7)$$

$$\frac{\partial L}{\partial \lambda} = 1 - Q_1 - 2Q_2 \qquad\qquad\qquad = 0 \qquad (4.8)$$

Multiplying (4.6) by Y_2/Y_1 and subtracting from (4.7) enables the following expression for λ to be obtained:

$$\lambda = \frac{Z_1 Y_2 - Z_2 Y_1}{Y_2 - 2Y_1} \qquad (4.9)$$

Substituting from (4.8) and (4.9) into (4.7) to solve for Q_2 gives:

$$2Y_1 Y_2 (1 - 2Q_2) + 2Y_2^2 Q_2 + 2(\frac{Z_1 Y_2 - Z_2 Y_1}{Y_2 - 2Y_1}) = Z_2$$

which may be re-written:

$$Q_2 (2Y_2^2 - 4Y_1 Y_2) = Z_2 - 2(\frac{Z_1 Y_2 - Z_2 Y_1}{Y_2 - 2Y_1}) - 2Y_1 Y_2 \qquad (4.10)$$

It is now possible to re-express (4.10) in terms of the decision variables of the original problem:

$$Q_2 (2(X_1 + X_2)^2 - 4X_1 (X_1 + X_2)) = X_1^2 + X_2^2 - 2\left\{ \frac{X_1^2 (X_1 + X_2) - (X_1^2 + X_2^2) X_1}{X_1 + X_2 - 2X_1} \right\}$$

$$- 2X_1 (X_1 + X_2)$$

$$Q_2(2X_2^2 - 2X_1^2) = X_1^2 + X_2^2 - 2\left\{\frac{X_1X_2(X_1 - X_2)}{X_2 - X_1}\right\} - 2X_1(X_1 + X_2)$$

$$= X_1^2 + X_2^2 + 2X_1X_2 - 2X_1^2 - 2X_1X_2$$

$$= X_2^2 - X_1^2$$

Therefore $Q_2 = \frac{1}{2}$ which implies $Q_1 = 0$, from (4.8). This result also holds for the special case when $Y_1 = 0$.

Hence for all X_1 and $X_2 (X_1 \neq X_2)$, the point of tangency between the objective function and the constraint line occurs at $Q_1 = 0$, $Q_2 = \frac{1}{2}$. But this is precisely the intersection point of the constraint line and the Q_2 axis. Thus, in the two dimensional case, there is a coincidence of the corner point and the tangent optimum at A. The two dimensional problem has its optimal solution at a corner point of the feasible region. The case where $X_1 = X_2$ is of no real interest as, in this case, the only two available strategies are indistinguishable in terms of their payoffs. It can easily be shown, by checking the second order conditions (see, e.g., Roberts and Schulze, 1973) that the optimum just located corresponds to maximum variance. Minimum variance occurs, without tangency, at B (Figure 4.2), as will be discussed more fully in the next section.

4.4 SOLUTION OF THE PROBLEM IN n DIMENSIONS (2)

Consider now the Lagrangian appropriate to the general problem:

$$L = \sum_{j=1}^{n} Z_j Q_j - (\sum_{j=1}^{n} Y_j Q_j)^2 + \lambda(1 - \sum_{j=1}^{n} jQ_j)$$

Again, ignoring temporarily the non-negativity constraints on the Q_j, for an optimum it is necessary that the $(n + 1)$ simultaneous linear equations formed from the partial derivatives of L with respect to the Q_j and to λ be soluble for n values of Q_j and one value of λ. That is, it must be possible to solve:

$$2 \sum_{i=1}^{n} Y_j Y_i Q_i + j\lambda = Z_j \quad (j=1....n) \qquad (4.11)$$

$$\sum_{j=1}^{n} jQ_j = 1 \qquad (4.12)$$

In n dimensions, it is no longer the case that optima of type C cannot exist. However, it will now be shown that, even if non-corner optima do exist, there will always be a corner optimum which yields the same value for Var (S), so that in practice, as in the expected value calculations, it is only necessary to consider corner optima. A corner optimum has only one $Q_j > 0$ and the remainder all zero.

Theorem 4.1 : A necessary and sufficient condition for (4.11) and (4.12) to be soluble is that there are at most two different payoff values. (That is, for j = 1....n, either $X_j = X_1$ or $(X_j - X_1)(X_j - X_t) = 0$, where t is the smallest integer such that $X_t \neq X_1$.)

Proof:

Case A : $X_j = X_1$ for all j.

(1) Necessity: Suppose (4.11) and (4.12) are soluble. $X_j = X_1$ for all j is not inconsistent with solubility, nor with Theorem 4.1.

(2) Sufficiency: If $X_j = X_1$ for all j, then $Y_j = jX_1$ and $Z_j = jX_1^2$. It is thus easily seen that (4.11) and (4.12) are soluble, yielding $\lambda = -X_1^2$. $X_j = X_1$ is a sufficient condition for (4.11) and (4.12) to be soluble.

If $X_j = X_1$ for all j, any probability distribution which satisfies (4.12) is a solution, the maximum and minimum variances are zero and the decision problem is trivial.

Case B : t is the smallest integer such that $2 \leqslant t \leqslant n$ and $X_t \neq X_1$.

Since for j = 1....(t-1), $Y_j = jX_1$ and $Z_j = jX_1^2$, each of the first (t-1) equations in (4.11) reduces to

$$2X_1 \sum_{i=1}^{n} Y_i Q_i + \lambda = X_1^2 \qquad\qquad (4.13)$$

Further, subtracting j times (4.13) from each of the equations j = t....n in (4.11) gives

$$2(Y_j - jX_1) \sum_{i=1}^{n} Y_i Q_i = Z_j - jX_1^2 \qquad (j = t....n) \qquad (4.14)$$

(4.13) and (4.14) are equivalent for Case B to (4.11)

(1) Necessity: Suppose (4.11) and (4.12) (equivalently (4.12), (4.13) and (4.14)) are soluble. Then if, for a given j = t....n, $Y_j - jX_1 = 0$, not only does $Y_j = jX_1$, but also $Z_j = jX_1^2$, from (4.14).

That is $X_1 = (\sum_{i=1}^{j} X_i)/j$

and $X_1^2 = (\sum_{i=1}^{j} X_i^2)/j$

Hence $(\sum_{i=1}^{j} X_i^2)/j - (\sum_{i=1}^{j} X_i/j)^2 = 0$

which implies that $X_j = X_1$ for all i = 1....j, which contradicts the assumption that $X_1 \neq X_t$. Hence $Y_j - jX_1 \neq 0$ for any j = t....n. As a result, (4.14) can be written

$$\sum_{i=1}^{n} Y_i Q_i = (Z_j - jX_1^2)/2(Y_j - jX_1)$$

$$= k \text{ (constant)} \qquad (j = t....n)$$

Further, by considering the case $j = t$, it is easily shown that
$k = (X_1 + X_t)/2$. Thus

$$Z_j - jX_1^2 = (X_1 + X_t)(Y_j - jX_1) \qquad (j = t....n)$$

Subtracting the equation for $(j-1)$ from each equation $j = (t+1)....n$
gives

$$X_j^2 - X_1^2 = (X_1 + X_t)(X_j - X_1) \qquad (j = t....n)$$

which implies $(X_j - X_1)(X_j - X_t) = 0$, not only for $j = t....n$, but also
for $j = 1....(t-1)$, by definition of t.

(2)<u>Sufficiency</u>: Suppose $(X_j - X_1)(X_j - X_t) = 0$ for $j = 1....n$. Let
$Y_j = a_jX_1 + (j-a_j)X_t$, where a_j is the number of occurrences of a payoff
of X_1 in the first j payoffs. Similarly, let $Z_j = a_jX_1^2 + (j-a_j)X_t^2$.
Substituting into (4.14) gives

$$2 (a_jX_1 + (j-a_j)X_t - jX_1) \sum_{i=1}^{n} Y_iQ_i = a_jX_1^2 + (j-a_j)X_t^2 - jX_1^2$$
$$(j = t....n)$$

Simplifying yields

$$2(j-a_j)(X_t - X_1) \sum_{i=1}^{n} Y_iQ_i = (j-a_j)(X_t^2 - X_1^2)$$

which implies

$$\sum_{i=1}^{n} Y_iQ_i = (X_1 + X_t)/2 \qquad (j = t....n)$$

Thus (4.11) and (4.12) reduce to three equations

$$2X_1(\sum_{i=1}^{n} Y_iQ_i) + \lambda = X_1^2 \qquad (4.15)$$

$$\sum_{i=1}^{n} Y_iQ_i = (X_1 + X_t)/2 \qquad (4.16)$$

$$\sum_{j=1}^{n} jQ_j = 1 \qquad (4.17)$$

Solving (4.15) and (4.16) yields $\lambda = -X_1X_t$. Also, it is clear that
(4.16) and (4.17) will always be soluble no matter what the values of
X_1 and X_t.

This completes the proof of Theorem 4.1. It has been shown that
restricting the number of distinct payoff values to no more than two is
both necessary and sufficient to ensure the existence of solutions to
(4.11) and (4.12).

<u>Theorem 4.2</u> : If for $j = 1....n$, $X_j = X_1$ or $X_j = X_t$ where t is any
integer such that $2 \leqslant t \leqslant n$, then $\frac{1}{4} (X_1 - X_t)^2$ is an upper bound on the

33

variance of strategy S. The upper bound is attained if and only if there exists a feasible probability distribution such that $P = \frac{1}{2}$ where P is the sum of the probabilities of all the states of nature having X_1 as payoff.

Proof:
$$Var(S) = \sum_{j=1}^{n} P_j X_j^2 - (\sum_{j=1}^{n} P_j X_j)^2$$

$$= P X_1^2 + (1 - P)X_t^2 - (P X_1 + (1 - P)X_t)^2$$

$$= P(1 - P)(X_1 - X_t)^2$$

By straightforward calculus, $P(1 - P) \leqslant \frac{1}{4}$ if $0 \leqslant P \leqslant 1$ and $P(1 - P) = \frac{1}{4}$ if and only if $P = \frac{1}{2}$. Thus Theorem 4.2 is proved.

Having shown that solutions to (4.11) and (4.12) do exist, and having obtained an upper bound on the associated variance, it is now necessary to show that non-corner solutions can exist, which also obey the inequality constraints (4.5). To do this the following definition and lemma are required:

Definition: A set $Q_1....Q_n$ is a basic solution if the values of the Q_j satisfy (4.16), (4.17) and (4.5) and no more than two Q_j's are strictly positive.

Lemma: If the feasible region defined by the constraints (4.16), (4.17) and (4.5) is bounded, then every solution to the system is a convex combination of the basic solutions.

The above is a well known result in linear programming, see, e.g., Vajda (1961).

The constraint set (4.16), (4.17) and (4.5) (equivalently (4.11), (4.12) and (4.5)) cannot define an unbounded feasible region since (4.17) and (4.5) imply the restrictions $0 \leqslant Q_j \leqslant 1/j (j = 1....n)$. Hence, given the preceding lemma, it is only necessary to consider basic solutions. Further, if, in any solution, $Q_r = 1/r$, all remaining Q_j must be zero (4.17). Thus for solutions which are non-corner solutions with respect to the original feasible region defined by (4.4) and (4.5), but which are also basic with respect to the feasible region for variance-optimising solutions defined by (4.16), (4.17) and (4.5) it is necessary for there to exist two integers, ℓ and r, in the range 1....n (inclusive) such that $0 < Q_\ell < 1/\ell$ and $0 < Q_r < 1/r$.

Finally, before seeking to establish the potential existence of non-corner solutions (Type C in Figure 4.1), it can be noted that, by subtracting X_1 times (4.17) from (4.16) and simplifying, (4.16), (4.17) and (4.5) may be replaced by

$$\sum_{j=t}^{n} (j - a_j)Q_j = \frac{1}{2} \qquad (4.18)$$

$$\sum_{j=1}^{n} jQ_j = 1 \qquad (4.19)$$

$$Q_j \geqslant 0 \quad (j = 1....n) \qquad (4.20)$$

34

Theorem 4.3 : A necessary and sufficient condition for the existence of a non-corner solution to (4.18), (4.19) and (4.20) is that at least one of the following conditions holds:

(i) there exists an integer h such that $t < h \leqslant n$ and $h > 2a_h$

(ii) there exist two distinct integers, ℓ and r such that $\ell = 2a_\ell$, $r = 2a_r$, $t \leqslant \ell \leqslant n$ and $t \leqslant r \leqslant n$.

Proof:

(1) Necessity: Suppose (4.18), (4.19) and (4.20) have a non-corner solution such that $Q_\ell > 0$, $Q_r > 0$, $Q_j = 0$ ($j = 1....n$, $j \neq \ell$, $j \neq r$). $\ell < r$, by assumption. For (4.18) to be satisfied, r must lie in the range t....n (inclusive).

Case A: $1 \leqslant \ell \leqslant t - 1$.

In this case, (4.18) and (4.19) become

$$2(r - a_r)Q_r = 1 \qquad\qquad (4.21)$$

$$\ell Q_\ell + r Q_r = 1 \qquad\qquad (4.22)$$

Subtracting (4.22) from (4.21) gives

$$- \ell Q_\ell + (r - 2a_r)Q_r = 0$$

which implies $r > 2a_r$ since $Q_\ell > 0$ and $Q_r > 0$. Hence it is possible, for example, to put h = r. Moreover, $r \neq t$, since if r = t, it is implied that $t > 2a_t = 2a_{t-1} = 2(t-1)$, which is impossible. Thus $t < h \leqslant n$.

Case B: $t \leqslant \ell \leqslant n$.

In this case, (4.18) and (4.19) become $\qquad\qquad (4.23)$

$$2(\ell - a_\ell)Q_\ell + 2(r - a_r)Q_r = 1$$

$$\ell Q_\ell + r Q_r = 1 \qquad\qquad (4.24)$$

Subtracting (4.24) from (4.23) gives

$$(\ell - 2a_\ell)Q_\ell + (r - 2a_r)Q_r = 0 \qquad\qquad (4.25)$$

Since $Q_\ell > 0$, $Q_r > 0$ and (4.25) holds, then

either (i) $\ell > 2a_\ell$ and $r < 2a_r$, in which case it is possible to set h = ℓ, or $\ell < 2a_\ell$ and $r > 2a_r$, in which case it is possible to set h = r. As in case A $t < h \leqslant n$.

or (ii) $\ell = 2a_\ell$ and $r = 2a_r$

35

(2) Sufficiency:

Case A: Suppose there exists an integer $h (t < h \leqslant n)$ such that $h > 2a_h$. Choosing any integer $\ell (1 \leqslant \ell \leqslant t-1)$ and setting $h = r$, (4.21) and (4.22) give

$$Q_\ell = \frac{h - 2a_h}{2\ell(h - a_h)}$$

$$Q_h = \frac{1}{2(h - a_h)}$$

$$Q_j = 0 \qquad\qquad (j = 1 \ldots n,\ j \neq \ell,\ j \neq h)$$

which is a non-corner solution to (4.18), (4.19) and (4.20).

Further, substituting into the expression for $\mathrm{Var}(S)$ gives

$$\mathrm{Var}(S) = \sum_{j=1}^{n} Z_j Q_j - (\sum_{j=1}^{n} Y_j Q_j)^2$$

$$= Z_\ell Q_\ell + Z_h Q_h - \tfrac{1}{4}(X_1 + X_t)^2 \qquad\qquad (\text{ from}(4.16))$$

$$= \ell X_1^2 Q_\ell + (a_h X_1^2 + (h - a_h)X_t^2)\, Q_h - \tfrac{1}{4}(X_1 + X_t)^2$$

(since $1 \leqslant \ell \leqslant t - 1$, $a_\ell = \ell$)

$$= (X_1^2(h-2a_h) + a_h X_1^2 + (h-a_h)X_t^2) / (2(h-a_h))$$

$$\qquad\qquad\qquad - \tfrac{1}{4}(X_1 + X_t)^2$$

(using the expressions just derived for Q_ℓ and Q_h)

$$= \tfrac{1}{4}(X_1 - X_t)^2, \text{ the upper bound.}$$

(by straightforward simplification)

Case B: Suppose there exist two distinct integers, ℓ and r lying in the range $t \ldots n$ (inclusive) and such that $\ell = 2a_\ell$ and $r = 2a_r$. Choosing any α such that $0 < \alpha < 1$, the set $Q_\ell = \alpha/\ell$, $Q_r = (1 - \alpha)/r$, $Q_j = 0$ $(j = 1 \ldots n,\ j \neq \ell,\ j \neq r)$ is a non-corner solution to (4.18), (4.19) and (4.20), as can be checked by direct substitution.

Also, the corresponding variance is again $\tfrac{1}{4}(X_1 - X_t)^2$, the upper bound.

Theorem 4.4 : Even when the set of equations (4.18), (4.19) and (4.20) has a non-corner solution, there will still exist a corner solution with variance $\tfrac{1}{4}(X_1 - X_t)^2$, the upper bound.

Proof: By definition, there exists a corner solution if for an integer g $(1 \leqslant g \leqslant n)$ the set $Q_g = 1/g$, $Q_j = 0$ $(j = 1 \ldots n,\ j \neq g)$ satisfies (4.18), which happens if, from (4.18), $t \leqslant g \leqslant n$ and $(g - a_g)Q_g = \tfrac{1}{2}$, i.e. $g = 2a_g$.

By substitution, the corresponding variance is

$$Var(S) = Z_g Q_g - (Y_g Q_g)^2$$

$$= \frac{a_g}{g}(X_1^2 + X_t^2) - (\frac{a_g}{g}(X_1 + X_t))^2$$

$$= \tfrac{1}{4}(X_1 - X_t)^2$$

Finally, to complete the proof it is necessary to show that if there is a non-corner solution, there will exist an appropriate integer g.

Suppose there exists a non-corner solution with $1 \leqslant \ell \leqslant t - 1$. Then, by Theorem 4.3, there exists an $h > 2a_h$ such that $t < h \leqslant n$. For $1 \leqslant \ell \leqslant t - 1$, $\ell = a_\ell < 2a_\ell$. But, eventually, there exists an $h > \ell$ such that $h > 2a_h$. Thus, somewhere in the range of subscripts t....w....n, a cross-over must occur such that

$$w \leqslant 2a_w \qquad\qquad\qquad (4.26)$$

$$w + 1 > 2a_{w+1} \qquad\qquad\qquad (4.27)$$

If $X_w = X_1$, $a_w = (a_{w+1} - 1)$ and (4.26) and (4.27) cannot hold. If $X_w = X_t$, $a_w = a_{w+1}$ and

$$w \leqslant 2a_{w+1}$$

$$w + 1 > 2a_{w+1}$$

which can only occur if $w = 2a_w$.

Suppose alternatively that there exists a non-corner solution with $t \leqslant \ell \leqslant n$. Then, by Theorem 4.3, one of three possibilities arises:

(a) (i) There exists an $\ell > 2a_\ell$ and an $r < 2a_r$.

In this case, since $\ell < r$ (by assumption), as ℓ increases, there must exist somewhere in the range $t \leqslant \ell \leqslant w \leqslant r \leqslant n$ a cross-over such that

$$w \geqslant 2a_w$$

$$w + 1 < 2a_{w+1}$$

which, by a similar argument to that previously advanced, can only occur if $w = 2a_w$.

(ii) There exists an $\ell < 2a_\ell$ and an $r > 2a_r$.

In this case, since $\ell < r$, as ℓ increases, there must exist somewhere in the range $t \leqslant \ell \leqslant w \leqslant r \leqslant n$ a cross-over such that

$$w \leqslant 2a_w$$

$$w + 1 > 2a_{w+1}$$

which can only occur if $w = 2a_w$.

37

(b)   There exists $\ell = 2a_\ell$ and $r = 2a_r$.

In this case g may be set equal ℓ or r.

Thus the proof of Theorem 4.4 is completed - even when there is a non-corner solution, there will always exist a corner solution with variance equal to the upper bound.

Theorems 4.1 - 4.4 jointly show that, in the n state of nature case, non-corner optima are possible, but only under restrictive conditions, and, even then, there will always be a corner point for which the value of Var(S) is equal to the upper bound. Effectively, since only two distinct payoffs are possible, the n-dimensional problem is being reduced to a problem of dimension two by grouping together the states of nature for which payoffs are the same.

Now it is also the case that the point which corresponds to minimum variance can be uniquely identified for all problems. Variance must, by definition, be non-negative and so the minimum possible variance is zero. This will occur when one state of nature, say j, occurs with certainty ($P_j = 1$) and all other states cannot occur ($P_k = 0$ for all $k \neq j$). Clearly, by examining the original ranking constraints, $P_j \geqslant P_{j+1}$ (j = 1....(n - 1)) , the zero variance case must be $P_1 = 1$; $P_2 = P_3 = ... = P_n = 0$. Because minimum variance is always zero, it is of no value for distinguishing between strategies. It follows that only maximum variance need be considered.

It also follows that the optimum which has been located through pursuing the tangency argument must correspond to the point of maximum variance. Moreover, since it has been shown that, even in the presence of non-corner optima, there is a corner point with the same, upper bound, value of variance, it can be concluded that, just as in the expected value problem investigated in the previous chapter, it is sufficient, in order to determine the maximum variance, to examine only corner points. A variance maximum must thus occur at the intersection of the constraint (4.19) and one of the axes, at which time, one Q_j will be positive and all the others zero. Clearly, from the constraint, the value of each Q_j will be 1/j and so the point of maximum variance is found by examining all expressions of the objective function:

$$
\begin{aligned}
\text{Var(S)} &= \frac{Z_j}{j} - (\frac{Y_j}{j})^2 \\
&= \frac{1}{j} \sum_{k=1}^{j} X_k^2 - (\frac{1}{j} \sum_{k=1}^{j} X_k)^2
\end{aligned}
\tag{4.28}
$$

for j = 1....n. (3)

If j* is the value of j which maximises Var(S), then $Q_{j*} = 1/j*$ and all other Q_j are zero. In terms of the original probabilities of states of nature this becomes:

$$P_1 = P_2 = ... = P_{j*} = 1/j* \; ; \; P_{j*+1} = P_{j*+2} = ... = P_n = 0.$$

It is these values of the P_j which, if they happened to occur, would give the largest variance for the distribution of payoffs of the strategy under investigation.

4.5 NUMERICAL EXAMPLE

To illustrate the techniques described in the preceding section,
consider the following hypothetical transport infrastructure investment
policy problem. Suppose two road investment strategies (A and B) are to
be compared whose net present values will depend principally upon two
factors, the future cost of fuel and government policy with regard to
urban traffic. For simplicity, assume that fuel costs may be either
"high" or "low" and government policy "favourable" or "unfavourable".
The possible payoffs of the two strategies are shown below:

<u>Strategy A</u>   <u>Strategy B</u>

         Unfavourable Favourable   Unfavourable Favourable

Low $X_{A4} = 18$ $X_{A3} = 26$ Low $X_{B4} = 10$ $X_{B3} = 22$

High $X_{A1} = 4$ $X_{A2} = 12$ High $X_{B1} = 6$ $X_{B2} = 8$

Figure 4.3 Payoffs for the Transport Infrastructure Problem

The figures associated with the payoffs, X_{ij}, corresponding to the
different possible combinations of future circumstances, are the net
present values (n.p.v.) of the returns which would accrue in each case,
measured in millions of pounds. Further, suppose that the probabilities
estimated <u>a priori</u> to be associated with each of the four possible
states of nature whose n.p.v's are X_{11}, X_{12}, X_{13} and X_{14} are P_1, P_2, P_3
and P_4 respectively and that these probabilities may be ranked $P_1 \geqslant P_2$
$\geqslant P_3 \geqslant P_4$.

First of all, to find the maximum and minimum n.p.v. of each strategy,
given the above restrictions on the P_j, equation (3.11) may be applied
to calculate the partial averages. It can readily be confirmed that
they are:

	1	2	3	4
Strategy A	4	8	14	15
Strategy B	6	7	12	11½

Thus, given the constraints on the P_j, the minimum expected n.p.v. for
A is £4m. and for B is £6m. The maximum expected n.p.v. for A is £15m.
and for B is £12m. Strategy A has the higher maximum expected n.p.v.,
but it also has a lower minimum. Clearly, the choice between the two
strategies is likely to be influenced by the decision maker's attitude
to risk. In such circumstances, one consideration which should be taken
into account is the likely dispersion of the distribution of strategy
n.p.v's, since a smaller expected dispersion will imply a greater
likelihood of an actual outcome close to the expected value. With this
in mind, maximum and minimum variances of payoff may be calculated.

For both strategies A and B, the minimum variance must be zero, as
explained in section 4.4. The maximum variance for each strategy is
found by computing the four partial variances, using equation (4.28).

For Strategy A we have:

$$j = 1: \qquad 16 - 16 \qquad\qquad\qquad = 0$$
$$j = 2: \qquad \tfrac{1}{2}(16 + 144) - 64 \qquad\qquad = 16$$
$$j = 3: \qquad \tfrac{1}{3}(16 + 144 + 676) - 196 \qquad = 82\tfrac{2}{3}$$
$$j = 4: \qquad \tfrac{1}{4}(16 + 144 + 676 + 324) - 225 = 65$$

For Strategy B, the corresponding results are:

$j =$	1	2	3	4
Partial Variance	0	1	$50\tfrac{2}{3}$	$38\tfrac{3}{4}$

Thus the maximum variance in n.p.v. for Strategy A is $82^2/_3$, giving a maximum standard deviation of 9.09. Therefore, whatever values the unknowns, P_j, actually take, it is known that the largest possible variance of the distribution of payoffs about the mean is $82^2/_3$ for Strategy A. Similarly for Strategy B, the largest possible variance of its distribution of payoffs about its mean is $50^2/_3$, i.e. a standard deviation of 7.12. In both cases it is clear that the standard deviation is high, even in relation to the maximum expected value of each strategy. Strategy B, however, although it has the lower maximum expected value, has a higher minimum expected value and a smaller variance. If the decision maker regards it as important to minimise the probability of making a really poor choice, then the analysis which has just been undertaken indicates that Strategy B will be the more appealing to him, even though the chances of an exceptionally good result are smaller than if Strategy A had been selected.

4.6 CONCLUSIONS

This chapter has demonstrated one form of extension to the original results on the determination of extreme expected values of a strategy. It is now possible to compare strategies not only on the basis of their expected payoffs, but also on the basis of the maximum variance of the distribution of payoffs. Alternatively, standard deviation could be used in place of variance, merely by taking the appropriate square root at the end of the computations. The ability to compare strategies both from the point of view of central tendency and dispersion is of real value, since in many situations it seems likely that decision makers will be prepared to sacrifice something in the way of expected returns for a greater certainty of achieving a result close to that expected. How that type of trade-off might be formalised is the subject of the next chapter.

NOTES

(1) This chapter is not concerned with the precise form of the trade-off, nor with the extent to which a measure of expected value, coupled with one of dispersion, adequately captures all relevant features of a distribution of payoffs. These questions are discussed in Chapter 5. Here it is merely implied that some information about

likely dispersion may assist decision making.

(2) This section draws heavily on Agunwamba (1981). The authors are glad to acknowledge the very valuable contribution Dr. Agunwamba's results have made to their understanding of the proof of this theorem.

(3) Equation 4.28 corresponds to a series of partial variances,directly analogous to the partial averages discussed in section 3.4.

5   Optimal strategy choice and expected value: variance trade-off

5.1   INTRODUCTION

The two preceding chapters have been concerned principally with
developing techniques for calculating respectively extreme expected
values of strategies and extreme variances. In particular, no attention
has yet been paid to the circumstances in which a decision maker may
wish to use both criteria simultaneously, nor to the manner in which he
may use them. In this chapter, these questions are examined in rather
more detail. Section 5.1 gives a brief account of some relevant
features of the theory of decision making under risk, especially the
von Neumann-Morgenstern cardinal utility measure. It is argued that,
although in some circumstances evaluation of a risky strategy can be
undertaken purely in terms of a single measure of expected utility, this
need not always be the case. In these circumstances, the joint
consideration of both expected value and dispersion can be appropriate,
and sections 5.2 and 5.3 describe two different ways in which this can
be done. Finally, section 5.4 examines the problems associated with
measures if dispersion about the mean which, unlike variance, attribute
greater weight to deviations one side of the mean than to the other.

5.2   THE EVALUATION OF RISKY STRATEGIES

Useful insights can be gained about the combination of variance and
expected value in decision making under conditions of incomplete
knowledge by considering why these two measures of strategy performance
have been utilised for assessment when the probabilities of the states
of nature are known precisely, i.e., in decision making under risk.
There is, in fact, a considerable body of theory concerned with the
question of strategy evaluation under risk. No attempt will be made to
cover it all, but only some of the most salient points will be
investigated.

   At the centre of the theory of decision making under risk lies the
von Neumann-Morgenstern cardinal utility measure. As mentioned in
section 2.7 the theory associated with this measure states that, if
certain intuitively plausible assumptions are made about the decision
maker's approach to assessing his preferences among strategies, then
strategies may be evaluated solely in terms of their expected utilities.
No reference to dispersion about the mean is required. The underlying
behavioural axioms have been expressed in a number of ways. What follows
is a broadly descriptive approach. For a more rigorous one see Arrow
(1970), or for an exposition embedded in the wider question of multiple
criteria decision making, Fishburn (1977).

A.   Ordering and Transitivity

A decision maker either prefers one of two risky strategies, S_1 and S_2,
or is indifferent between them. Such orderings are also transitive.

That is, if S_1 is preferred or regarded as indifferent to S_2 and similarly S_2 is preferred or is regarded as indifferent to S_3, then S_1 must be preferred or regarded as indifferent to S_3.

B. Continuity

If a decision maker prefers S_1 to S_2 to S_3, then a subjective probability $P(1)(\neq 0 \text{ or } 1)$ exists such that he is indifferent between S_2 and a lottery yielding S_1 with probability $P(1)$ and S_3 with probability $1 - P(1)$.

C. Independence

If S_1 is preferred to S_2, and S_3 is any other risky strategy, a lottery with S_1 and S_3 as its outcomes will be preferred to a lottery with S_2 and S_3 as outcomes when $P(1) = P(2)$. That is, preference between S_1 and S_2 is independent of S_3.

From these three axioms, what is termed Bernoulli's principle may be deduced. They are necessary and sufficient conditions for the existence of a utility function, U, which associates a single real number (a utility value) with any risky strategy, where U has the following properties:
(a) If S_1 is preferred to S_2 then $U(S_1) > U(S_2)$ and vice versa (where $U(S_i)$ is to be understood as the utility value of S_i).
(b) The utility of a risky strategy is its expected utility value, the expectation being based on the deicision maker's subjective probability distribution of outcomes, i.e.,

$$U(S_i) = \sum_{j=1}^{n} U(S_i | N_j) \, P_j$$

Also, importantly, higher moments of utility (e.g., variance) are not relevant to decision making.
(c) The scale on which utility is defined is only unique up to a positive linear transformation, i.e. U is measured on an interval scale. There is no absolute scale of utility and thus comparison of utility values between individuals is meaningless.

The above are a very powerful set of results based, as they are, on a small and straightforward set of plausible behavioural axioms. The axioms imply the existence of both a utility function which reflects the decision maker's preferences and a subjective probability distribution for states of nature. Further, in such circumstances, the maximisation of expected utility is the only criterion of strategy choice which should be considered.

Clearly, if the von Neumann-Morgenstern axioms could be accepted, and the implied methodology adopted, in all cases, then the consideration given in chapter 4 to the calculation of extreme variances would be redundant. As section 2.7 has already indicated, however, there are at least two sets of circumstances in which the von Neumann-Morgenstern approach may be inoperable. The first is when the payoffs, X_{ij}, of given strategy/state of nature combinations are not measured in utility terms, but in some other units, for example, money units. If, for any reason, X_{ij}'s cannot be expressed as utilities, then the remainder of the von Neumann-Morgenstern approach no longer follows automatically - in particular, there is no implication that expected monetary payoff alone is a complete measure of a value of a strategy. Secondly, even if payoff measurement in utility units is feasible, there are some objections to the implications of the behavioural axioms which form the basis of the von Neumann-Morgenstern conclusions.

Details of some of the objections which have been raised may be found in Allais (1955); Thrall (1954); Luce (1956); Fishburn (1972,1976) and Slovic and Tversky (1974). It is beyond the scope of the present discussion to investigate the nature of all of them. Allais', however, is perhaps the most straightforward and is explained in section 2.7. Although some would argue that his criticism is misplaced, there is sufficient room for doubt, especially in the light of the other objections to the von Neumann-Morgenstern approach, to justify the examination, within the incomplete knowledge context, of approaches to strategy choice which do take into account measures of the dispersion of payoffs, as well as expected value.

5.3 EXPECTED VALUE: VARIANCE TRADE-OFFS USING INDIFFERENCE CURVE ANALYSIS

If, for whatever reason, the decision maker feels he should take into account both a measure of central tendency and a measure of dispersion in strategy choice, then, under incomplete knowledge, the most straightforward approach is to think in terms of some type of direct trade-off. For example, maximum or minimum expected payoff (or some combination of the two) might be traded off against maximum variance (or standard deviation, which may be preferable as it is measured in the same units as expected value). A large variance might be regarded as undesirable, indicating that a strategy possesses payoffs differing substantially from its expected value. It could also be viewed as a measure of inaccuracy or uncertainty associated with the estimated worth of a strategy, as measured by its expected value. A decision maker might well prefer a strategy with a slightly lower expected value to a competing strategy, if it also has a lower variance. The exact nature of the trade-off between the two factors will depend upon the decision maker's subjective evaluation of them. In practice, analysis might be undertaken using indifference curves similar in type, though not necessarily in outward appearance, to those used in elementary consumer theory in economics.

The shape of such indifference curves will depend upon the decision maker's marginal valuation of the two factors. If, for example he values a unit increase in maximum standard deviation as equivalent to a unit increase in an expected payoff measure, 'indifference curves' will be upward sloping 45° lines, see Figure 5.1. Thus Strategy A is preferable to Strategy B, since they both are rated the same in terms of expected payoff, but A has a lower maximum standard deviation. Similarly, C is preferable to both A and B.[1]

It has been implicit in the discussion so far that high variability is undesirable and low variability desirable. This reflects the conventional wisdom of decision theory which deprecates uncertainty. However, it could well be argued that, for example, a cautious decision maker who uses maximin expected value criterion might favour strategies with large rather than with small standard deviations. In this case the slope of the indifference curves would be quite different from that

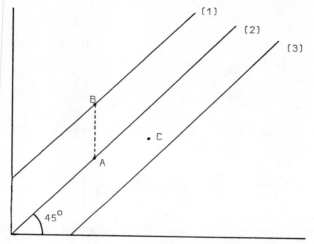

Figure 5.1 Trade-off Indifference Lines

implicit so far, being negative rather than positive. The reasoning
underlying the possible desirability of high standard deviation is the
implication that the strategy concerned has a relatively high probability
of a large deviation from its expected value. This in turn implies the
possibility of an outcome very much higher than expectation. If the
maximin decision maker feels that his caution is already adequately
reflected in his expected value criterion, he may be willing to accept
some risk in respect of variability thereby moderating his overall
attitude to uncertainty. Whether decision makers do in fact behave in
this way is an empirical question beyond the scope of the present
chapter.

5.4 INCORPORATION OF EXPECTED VALUE AND VARIANCE INTO A SINGLE INDEX

The approach to the consideration of both central tendency and dispersion
in strategy assessment suggested in the previous paragraph uses an index
of expected value and a maximum variance (or standard deviation) which
are independently calculated. As a result, it is possible that the sets
of probabilities of states of nature underlying the two independent
calculations need not be the same. Although it is quite plausible that
the decision maker might approach strategy evaluation on the basis of
independent calculations, it does suggest that he be required to maintain
two mutually inconsistent views of the probability distribution of states
of nature.

To avoid this difficulty it is worthwhile to investigate a second
approach to the joint consideration of expected value and variance. (2)
In this approach, the two are combined into a single index, on the
assumption that they are traded off against each other linearly. Let

45

$\bar{X}$ represent expected value and V represent variance. Then the index of strategy value, I, can be written as

$$I = \bar{X} + bV \qquad (5.1)$$

where, since only the ranking of I values for different strategies is of any consequence, only a single parameter, b, reflecting the rate of $\bar{X}$, V trade-off is required in the expression for I. b is likely to be negative in most applications, implying risk aversion on the part of the decision maker. Assuming now, as in previous chapters, that states of nature are ranked $P_1 \geqslant P_2 \geqslant \ldots \geqslant P_n$, then the identification of maximum and minimum values of I to assist in strategy choice can be computed following a similar approach to that used in the calculation of variance extrema in chapter 4.

Since $\quad I = \bar{X} + bV$

$$= \sum_{j=1}^{n} P_j X_j + b\left\{ \sum_{j=1}^{n} P_j X_j^2 - \left(\sum_{j=1}^{n} P_j X_j \right)^2 \right\}$$

the question of finding extreme values of I can, using the transformations employed in chapters 3 and 4, be expressed formally as

<u>Maximise or Minimise</u>

$$I = \sum_{j=1}^{n} (Y_j + bZ_j) Q_j - b \left(\sum_{j=1}^{n} Y_j Q_j \right)^2$$

<u>subject to</u>

$$\sum_{j=1}^{n} jQ_j = 1$$

$$Q_j \geqslant 0 \qquad (j = 1 \ldots n)$$

I, it can be seen, is a quadratic function of the Q_j's, which suggests that its extreme values might well be located by adopting an approach similar to that used in chapter 4 with respect to variance.

On this occasion, consider first the n-dimensional case. The relevant Lagrangian is

$$L = \sum_{j=1}^{n} (Y_j + bZ_j)Q_j - b\left(\sum_{j=1}^{n} Y_j Q_j \right)^2 + \psi(1 - \sum_{j=1}^{n} jQ_j)$$

Ignoring temporarily the non-negativity constraints on the Q_j, for an optimum it is necessary that the (n+1) simultaneous linear equations formed from the partial derivatives of L with respect to the Q_j and to ψ be soluble for n values of Q_j and one value of ψ. That is, it must be possible to solve:

$$2b \sum_{i=1}^{n} Y_j Y_i Q_i + j\psi = Y_j + bZ_j \quad (j = 1 \ldots n) \qquad (5.2)$$

$$\sum_{j=1}^{n} jQ_j = 1 \qquad (5.3)$$

THEOREM 5.1:

A necessary and sufficient condition for (5.2) and (5.3) to be soluble is that there are at most two different payoff values.

Proof:

Case A: $X_j = X_1$ for all j

(1) Necessity: Suppose (5.2) and (5.3) are soluble. $X_j = X_1$ for all j is not inconsistent with solubility, nor with Theorem 5.1.
(2) Sufficiency: If $X_j = X_1$ for all j, then $Y_j = jX_1$ and $Z_j = jX_1^2$. Thus (5.2) and (5.3) are soluble, yielding $\psi = X_1 - bX_1^2$.

Case B: t is the smallest integer such that $2 \le t \le n$ and $X_t \ne X_1$. Since for $j = 1....(t-1)$, $Y_j = jX_1$ and $Z_j = jX_1^2$, each of the first $(t-1)$ equations in (5.2) reduces to

$$2bX_1 \sum_{i=1}^{n} Y_i Q_i + \psi = X_1 + bX_1^2 \qquad (5.4)$$

Further, subtracting j times (5.4) from each of the equations $j = t....n$ in (5.2) gives

$$2b(Y_j - jX_1) \sum_{i=1}^{n} Y_i Q_i = Y_j - jX_1 + b(Z_j - jX_1^2) \quad (j = t....n)$$

$$(5.5)$$

(1) Necessity: Suppose (5.2) and (5.3) (equivalently (5.3), (5.4) and (5.5)) are soluble. Then if, for a given $j = t....n$

$$Y_j - jX_1 = 0, \text{ not only does } Y_j = jX_1 \text{ but also}$$

$$Z_j = jX_1^2, \text{ from (5.5) which implies}$$

$$X_1 = (\sum_{i=1}^{j} X_i)/j$$

$$X_1^2 = (\sum_{i=1}^{j} X_i^2)/j$$

which, as in the equivalent stage in the variance proof in chapter 4 contradicts the assumption $X_1 \ne X_t$. Hence (5.5) can be written

$$\sum_{i=1}^{n} Y_i Q_i = \frac{Y_j - jX_1 + b(Z_j - jX_1^2)}{2b(Y_j - jX_1)}$$

$$= m \text{ (constant)} \qquad (j = t....n).$$

By considering the case $j = t$ it can be shown that

$$m = \frac{1 + b(X_t + X_1)}{2b}$$

Thus $(Y_j - jX_1)(1 + b(X_t + X_1)) = Y_j - jX_1 + b(Z_j - jX_1^2)(j = t....n)$

47

Subtracting the equation for $(j = 1)$ from each equation $j = (t+1)....n$ gives $(X_j - X_1)(X_j - X_t) = 0$, not only for $j = t....n$, but also for $j = 1....(t-1)$, by definition of t.

(2) Sufficiency: Suppose $(X_j - X_1)(X_j - X_t) = 0$ for $j = 1....n$.

Let $Y_j = a_j X_1 + (j - a_j)X_t$, where a_j is the number of occurrences of a payoff X_1 in the first j payoffs. Similarly, let $Z_j = a_j X_1^2 + (j-a_j)X_t^2$. Substituting into (5.5) gives

$$2b \left(a_j X_1 + (j - a_j)X_t - jX_1\right) \sum_{i=1}^{n} Y_i Q_i = a_j X_1 + (j - a_j)X_t - jX_1$$

$$+ b \left(a_j X_1^2 + (j - a_j)X_t^2 - jX_1^2\right) \qquad (j = t....n)$$

Simplifying yields $\displaystyle\sum_{i=1}^{n} Y_i Q_i = \frac{1 + b(X_t + X_1)}{2b}$ $\qquad (j = t....n)$

Thus (5.2) and (5.3) reduce to three equations

$$2bX_1 \sum_{i=1}^{n} Y_i Q_i + \psi = X_1 + bX_1^2 \qquad\qquad (5.6)$$

$$\sum_{i=1}^{n} Y_i Q_i = \frac{1 + b(X_t + X_1)}{2b} \qquad\qquad (5.7)$$

$$\sum_{i=1}^{n} jQ_j = 1 \qquad\qquad (5.8)$$

Solving (5.6) and (5.7) yields $\psi = - bX_1 X_t$. Also, (5.7) and (5.8) will always be soluble, no matter what the values of X_1 and X_t.

This completes the proof of Theorem 5.1. Restricting the number of distinct payoffs to no more than two is both necessary and sufficient to ensure the existence of solutions to (5.2) and (5.3).

So far, the investigation of the combined mean and variance index, I, has closely followed the pattern of chapter 4 when considering variance alone. However, a counter-example can easily be developed to show that the parallel cannot be taken further since, with the index I, although the existence of a maximum of two payoff values is necessary and sufficient for the existence of non-corner optima, it is now no longer the case that there will always be a corner optimum of equal value.

Counter-example: Consider a strategy for which, by Theorem 5.1, internal optima will exist

	N_1	N_2	N_3	N_4	N_5
S	1	4	4	4	1

and where mean:variance trade-off is of the form $I = \bar{X} - 3V$.

To find the extreme values of I, it is necessary to solve the problems:

Maximise or Minimise $\quad I = \sum_{j=1}^{5} (Y_j - 3Z_j)Q_j + 3\left(\sum_{j=1}^{5} Y_j Q_j\right)^2$

subject to $\qquad\qquad\qquad \sum_{j=1}^{5} jQ_j = 1$

$$Q_j \geqslant 0 \qquad\qquad (j = 1....5)$$

Corner solutions occur when $Q_j = 1/j$ $(j = 1....5)$ with all Q_k $(j \neq k)$ taking the value zero, and can be evaluated by the partial averaging approach used in the two previous chapters. Thus it is easily confirmed that the corner solutions are

j	1	2	3	4	5
I	1	$-4\frac{1}{4}$	-3	$-4\frac{1}{4}$	$-4^7/_{25}$

However, it is also readily shown that, in this case, an internal optimum exists which lies outside the range defined by the extreme members of the set of corner solutions.

As in Theorem 4.2, assume that P is the sum of the probabilities associated with all the states of nature having X_1 as payoff. Then I may be written as

$$I = \bar{X} + bV$$

$$= \sum_{j=1}^{n} P_j X_j + b\left\{ \sum_{j=1}^{n} P_j X_j^2 - \left(\sum_{j=1}^{n} P_j X_j \right)^2 \right\}$$

$$= PX_1 + (1 - P)X_t + b\left\{ PX_1^2 + (1 - P)X_t^2 \right.$$
$$\left. - (PX_1 + (1 - P)X_t)^2 \right\}$$

which simplifies to

$$I = PX_1 + (1 - P)X_t + bP(1 - P)(X_1 - X_t)^2$$

Ignoring temporarily the constraints on P implied by its interpretation as a probability, an internal optimum of I with respect to P requires

$$\frac{dI}{dP} = X_1 - X_t + b(X_1 - X_t)^2(1 - 2P) = 0$$

which implies $\qquad 1 + b(X_1 - X_t)(1 - 2P) = 0$

$$P = \tfrac{1}{2} + \frac{1}{2b(X_1 - X_t)} \qquad (5.9)$$

A second differentiation of I with respect to P shows that the above expression for P will yield a maximum for I if b is positive and a minimum if b is negative. In the particular numerical example under consideration, substitution gives a value $P = {}^5/_9$ which in turn gives a

49

value of $I = -4^1/_3$ which lies outside the range $-4^7/_{25}$ to $+1$ defined by the corner points.

Thus it may be concluded that the assessment of the extreme values of a linear combination, I, of mean and variance must proceed in the following way. Firstly, if there are more than two distinct payoffs, only corner points can be optimal. These may be identified by the simple partial average approach, applied to the amended objective function. If there are only two distinct payoff values, however, the <u>possibility</u> of one of the extremes being internal exists. For positive b it would be the maximum; for negative b, the minimum. However, depending on the relationship between b, X_1 and X_t, it need not always be the case that a feasible non-corner optimum can be identified. For example, the set $(b, X_1, X_t) = (\frac{1}{4}, 3, 7)$ yields $P = 0$ in (5.9) which is unacceptable since the minimum payoff associated with the first state of nature (which has a payoff X_1) is $1/_n$. If the value of P which maximises I cannot correspond to a feasible set of P_j values, then, again, a corner solution, identified by partial averaging, will be optimal. Finally, if the problem has only two states of nature, with distinct payoffs, the same approach must be adopted, recognising the possibility of a non-corner optimum. Unlike variance, it is not necessary that the values of the P_j which give a tangential optimum will automatically coincide with a corner point.

Thus, although a little more complicated than either the mean or variance optimisation problems, tackled in isolation, it has been shown that, if a decision maker wishes to consider the optimisation of a linear function of mean and variance, simple partial averaging will again normally suffice to locate the optimum. When it does not, the required computations are still quite straightforward.

Finally, it is worth noting that the use of the index, I, investigated in this section is not equivalent to applying any kind of quadratic utility function, $U_{ij} = aX_{ij}^2 + bX_{ij} + c$ to the individual's payoffs. Suppose, however, that a decision maker is prepared to convert individual payoffs to utilities using a function $U = f(X)$ of degree two or higher. This implicitly gives some significance to dispersion of payoffs about the mean payoff when expected utilities are calculated, since E(U) will involve terms of the form $\sum_{j=1}^{n} P_j X^k$, where $k \geqslant 2$. In these circumstances, assuming that the von Neumann-Morgenstern arguments on the use of expected value alone cannot for some reason be accepted, all that is necessary is to apply the standard partial averaging techniques to the U_{ij} in each strategy, as in chapters 3 and 4 and earlier in this section, rather than to the X_{ij}.

5.5 THE USE OF ASYMMETRIC MEASURES OF DISPERSION

Given that most decision makers may be regarded as being averse to unfavourable risks, and therefore keener to avoid negative deviations about the mean than positive ones, it is appropriate, finally in this chapter, to investigate the possibility of using measures of dispersion which, unlike the variance measure used in previous sections, give more favourable status to positive deviations than to equivalent negative ones. Unfortunately, it turns out that little useful progress can be made.

The only analytically malleable deviation index commonly used is variance, $\sum_{j=1}^{n} P_j(X_j - \bar{X})^2$. Since P_j reflects merely relative frequency of occurrence, the variance measure can be viewed as giving a weight $(X_j - \bar{X})$ to deviations of size $(X_j - \bar{X})$. In general application, this has the great advantage of making all terms $P_j(X_j - \bar{X})^2$ positive, so that any deviation from the mean, irrespective of direction, contributes straightforwardly to the measure of dispersion. A number of alternative weighting functions are graphed in Figure 5.2:

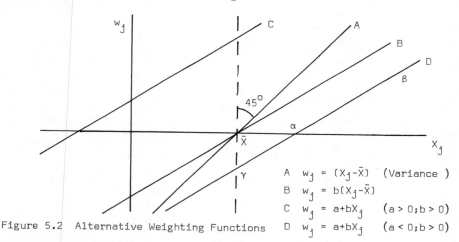

A $\quad w_j = (X_j - \bar{X})$ (Variance)
B $\quad w_j = b(X_j - \bar{X})$
C $\quad w_j = a + bX_j \quad (a > 0; b > 0)$
Figure 5.2 Alternative Weighting Functions D $\quad w_j = a + bX_j \quad (a < 0; b > 0)$

B gives an index of dispersion which is a simple multiple, b, of variance and so is of no new significance. C and D, however, have some potential interest as they do not give equal weighting to deviations of equal size on opposite sides of $X_j = \bar{X}$, although they have the disadvantage of not giving zero weighting to $X_j = \bar{X}$, a zero deviation observation. Consider D. A weighting function of this kind implies that in section $\alpha\beta$ positive weightings are given to positive $(X_j - \bar{X})$'s, the weighting increasing with the size of the deviation. In $\gamma\alpha$, negative weightings are given. This implies that <u>small</u> positive deviations are regarded as a definitely good thing since they are weighted so as to diminish the index of dispersion, which, conventionally, is regarded as desirable. Clearly, in the event of a decision maker positively desiring high deviation, adjustments to the weighting function would be required. The cut-off point between good (small) positive deviations and large (bad) ones depends on the parameters a and b. To the left of γ, negative deviations are given negative weights, so increasing the dispersion index. That is, negative deviations are regarded as bad and the bigger the deviation, the worse. This seems intuitively a reasonable weighting policy. It implies that distributions with small dispersions and with a preponderance of small positive deviations will be favoured over those with tendencies towards large and/or negative deviations.

However, considering the optimisation of a measure of deviation based on D gives the following results:

$$\underline{\text{Maximise/Minimise}} \quad \sum_{j=1}^{n} P_j w_j (X_j - \bar{X})$$

$$= \sum_{j=1}^{n} P_j (a + bX_j)(X_j - \bar{X})$$

$$= a \sum_{j=1}^{n} P_j X_j - a\bar{X} \sum_{j=1}^{n} P_j + b \sum_{j=1}^{n} P_j X_j^2 - b\bar{X} \sum_{j=1}^{n} P_j X_j$$

$$= b \left\{ \sum_{j=1}^{n} P_j X_j^2 - (\sum_{j=1}^{n} P_j X_j)^2 \right\}$$

This is just b times the variance and so will be maximised and minimised by the same P_j values as were fixed for the variance extrema. Similarly, the value of the intercept term, a, is unimportant. Hence there will be no difference in this respect between weighting functions C and D. Linear non-symmetric weighting functions do not therefore appear to be very interesting.

There are also some possibilities for non-linear functions, for example, quadratics and cubics, as illustrated in Figure 5.3. The cubic function has the effect of giving relatively heavy weight to larger deviations of either sign. It need not be symmetric with respect to the treatment of positive and negative deviations, although the illustration in Figure 5.3(a) is. The quadratic function in Figure 5.3(b) weights positive deviations less heavily than equal sized negative deviations. However, this leads to a deviation index which is a cubic function of the P_j. Although this function can be transformed into a relatively simple equation, endeavours to treat this dispersion index in the same way as variance have not proved successful. It seems probable that non-corner optima will frequently occur, so that no straightforward method for deriving extreme values of the measure would be available.

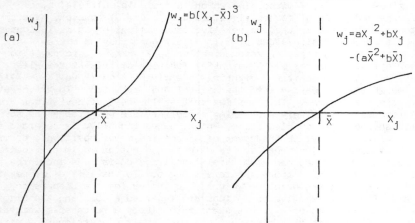

Figure 5.3(a) A Cubic Weighting Function, (b) A Quadratic Weighting
Function

Unfortunately, then, it seems that non-linear weightings are unable to provide useful results. If quadratic weighting is difficult to analyse, higher order weightings are likely to be even worse.

The final possibility is a linear function which "bends" at $X_j = \bar{X}$. This is easy to visualise, see Figure 5.4, but attempts to put it into

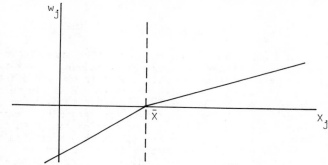

Figure 5.4 A Kinked Linear Weighting Function

programming form either via transformations or separable programming techniques all seem to lead to large constraint sets which will not be capable of straightforward non-algorithmic manipulation.

Overall, although there is a clear prima facie case in decision making for taking a deliberately asymmetric view of deviations about the mean (see Fisher and Hall, 1969 for some supporting empirical evidence), in practice, within the incomplete knowledge framework, no simple asymmetric indices of dispersion appear to be available.

NOTES

(1) It is, of course, also possible that the indifference curves are non-linear, either concave from below or above, depending on the decision maker's marginal valuation of the two factors.

(2) Since variance is measured in different units from the expected value, it may be preferable to consider as an index a linear combination of expected value and standard deviation. Agunwamba (1980) has shown that the extreme values of such an expression can be found using a partial averaging approach similar to those developed in chapters 3 and 4.

6 Sensitivity analysis of the basic results

6.1 INTRODUCTION

Chapters 3 and 4 were mainly concerned with the derivation of maximum
and minimum expected payoffs and maximum variances for strategies in a
situation where the decision maker is unable to specify exactly the
probabilities with which the states of nature are likely to occur, but
is able to rank them. The use of these results in decision making was
discussed in chapter 5. The aim of this chapter is to investigate the
sensitivity of the results obtained in chapters 3 and 4 to changes in
the assumptions on which they are based. In many real situations the
decision maker may be uncertain whether he has ranked the probabilities
of the states of nature correctly, and may want to know to what extent
will the initially obtained results change when the ranking is altered.
He may also want to introduce a new state of nature, which he had
previously ignored or overlooked, to see whether the initial results
will be materially affected. These problems are discussed in section
6.2. Moreover in most realistic decision situations, the payoff
corresponding to a particular combination of strategy and state of nature
will not be single valued, as was assumed so far, but may take different
values depending on a number of factors which may influence the final
outcome, e.g. the profitability of an investment project may be
influenced by changes in fashion for the product made, but such changes
may not be designated as separate states of nature. The influence of
variation in payoffs on choice of strategy is discussed in sections 6.3
and 6.4.

6.2 CHANGES IN THE PROBABILITY RANKING AND ADDITION OF NEW STATES OF NATURE

In determining the basic results of chapters 3 and 4, only a single
ranking of probabilities of states of nature was considered. In reality
this is unlikely to be the case in many situations, as the decision
maker may be uncertain about the probability ranking of some states of
nature. He may also introduce new states of nature, which he was
prepared to ignore initially, either because they were unlikely to occur
or because it was more convenient to amalgamate them with other states
of nature. In both cases it is of interest to investigate whether
general results are available which will indicate if the originally
obtained maximum and minimum expected values and maximum variance of a
strategy will change, and if so by how much. If this can be done, it
will not be necessary to calculate partial averages and variances ab
initio. It turns out that it is possible to derive general results for
certain types of ranking changes and for the introduction of new states
of nature.

Consider, in the first instance, the sensitivity of an initial evaluation of the extreme expected payoffs of a single strategy to the simplest possible ranking change, i.e., an inversion of the ranking of two consecutive states of nature. Suppose two states of nature, ranked j and (j + 1) are inverted. Of the n partial averages, only one will change, the jth. Let $\bar{X}_j'$ be the new jth partial average. Then

$$\bar{X}_j' = \frac{1}{j}(X_1 + \ldots + X_{j-1} + X_{j+1}) = \bar{X}_j + \frac{1}{j}(X_{j+1} - X_j) \qquad (6.1)$$

Thus, if $\bar{X}_j$ was not previously extremal, inverting two adjacent states of nature, j and j+1, will be immaterial, unless the difference between $\bar{X}_j$ and the original extreme partial average, $\bar{X}_{j*}$, was less than $\frac{1}{j}(X_{j+1} - X_j)$ in modulus, and unless $\bar{X}_j$ has changed to become more extreme. When this happens, $\bar{X}_j'$ will become the new maximum or minimum expected value. If $\bar{X}_j$ was previously extremal, there are two possibilities. Firstly, the jth partial average may remain extremal, but with a new extreme expected value given by $\bar{X}_j'$. Alternatively, if the difference between $\bar{X}_j$ and the next most extreme of the original partial averages was less than $\frac{1}{j}(X_{j+1} - X_j)$ in modulus, and if $\bar{X}_j$ has changed so as to become less extreme, then this nearest partial average takes over as the relevant extremum.

A similar effect can be traced for maximum variance, since this is located on the basis of a series of partial variance calculations, like those used to determine extreme expected payoffs. Continuing with the above case the new partial variance, V_j', for the jth state of nature is given by:

$$V_j' = \frac{1}{j}(X_1^2 + \ldots + X_{j-1}^2 + X_{j+1}^2) - (\frac{1}{j}(X_1 + \ldots + X_{j-1} + X_{j+1}))^2$$

$$= \frac{1}{j}(X_1^2 + \ldots + X_j^2) + \frac{1}{j}(X_{j+1}^2 - X_j^2) - (\frac{1}{j}(X_1 + \ldots + X_j)$$
$$+ \frac{1}{j}(X_{j+1} - X_j))^2$$

$$= \frac{1}{j}(X_1^2 + \ldots + X_j^2) + \frac{1}{j}(X_{j+1}^2 - X_j^2) - (\frac{1}{j}(X_1 + \ldots + X_j))^2$$
$$- \frac{2}{j^2}(X_1 + \ldots + X_j)(X_{j+1} - X_j) - (\frac{1}{j}(X_{j+1} - X_j))^2$$

$$= V_j + \frac{1}{j}(X_{j+1}^2 - X_j^2) - \frac{2}{j}(X_{j+1} - X_j)\bar{X}_j - (\frac{1}{j}(X_{j+1} - X_j))^2$$

$$(6.2)$$

Expression (6.2) does not appear to simplify to any appreciable extent. Again, if V_j was not previously maximal, inverting two adjacent states of nature, j and j+1, will not affect the maximum variance, unless $V_j' > V_j$ and the difference between V_j and the previous largest partial variance, V_{j*}, was less than $(V_j' - V_j)$. When this happens, V_j' will become the new maximum partial variance. If V_j was previously maximal, there are two possibilities. When $V_j' > V_j$, the jth partial variance remains maximal, but with a new value V_j'. When $V_j' < V_j$, the jth partial variance will remain maximal if V_j' is still larger than the unchanged partial variances. If this is not so, the next largest partial variance takes its place.

It is also possible to consider what happens when two non-adjacent states of nature, g and h, change positions in the ranking, where $g < h$. Such a change affects the partial averages $\bar{X}_g \ldots \bar{X}_{h-1}$ which have to be recalculated. The difference between the new and old partial averages will be $\bar{X}'_k - \bar{X}_k = \frac{1}{k}(X_h - X_g)$ for $k = g \ldots (h - 1)$. All these new partial averages will need to be compared with those unaffected by the inversion. New maximum and minimum expected payoffs may then be located.

Maximum variance will be affected similarly. It is necessary to recalculate the partial variances $V_g \ldots V_{h-1}$. This may be done using the following result, where V'_k is a new partial variance:

$$V'_k = V_k + \frac{1}{k}(X_h^2 - X_g^2) - \frac{2}{k}(X_h - X_g)\bar{X}_k - \left(\frac{1}{k}(X_h - X_g)\right)^2 \qquad (6.3)$$

for $k = g \ldots (h - 1)$, c.f. result (6.2). The new maximum variance is then located by inspection of the new and old partial variances.

Probability rankings may also be changed in a different way, by the introduction of a new state of nature with payoff X_N and ranked in the gth position. Partial averages $\bar{X}_1 \ldots \bar{X}_{g-1}$ will be unchanged, but all subsequent partial averages will change as follows. Let terms X' correspond to the new ranked set of payoffs, including X_N. Then

$$\bar{X}'_k = \frac{1}{k}(X'_1 + \ldots + X'_{g-1} + X'_g + X'_{g+1} + \ldots X'_k)$$

$$= \frac{1}{k}(X_1 + \ldots + X_{g-1} + X_N + X_g + \ldots + X_{k-1})$$

$$= \frac{1}{k}(X_1 + \ldots + X_k) + \frac{1}{k}(X_N - X_k)$$

$$= \bar{X}_k + \frac{1}{k}(X_N - X_k)$$

for $k = g \ldots n$. \qquad (6.4)

Also, $\bar{X}'_{n+1} = \frac{1}{n+1}(X_1 + \ldots X_{g-1} + X_N + X_g + \ldots + X_n)$. \qquad (6.5)

New partial averages are calculated as above, using expressions (6.4) and (6.5) and new extrema located by inspection of all (n+1) results.

Maximum variance may also change in these circumstances.

$$V'_k = \frac{1}{k}(X_1'^2 + \ldots + X_{g-1}'^2 + X_g'^2 + X_{g+1}'^2 + \ldots + X_k'^2)$$

$$- \left(\frac{1}{k}(X'_1 + \ldots + X'_{g-1} + X'_g + X'_{g+1} + \ldots + X'_k)\right)^2$$

$$= V_k + \frac{1}{k}(X_N^2 - X_k^2) - \frac{2}{k}(X_N - X_k)\bar{X}_k - \left(\frac{1}{k}(X_N - X_k)\right)^2 \qquad (6.6)$$

for $k = g \ldots n$, c.f. result (6.3).

$$V'_{n+1} = \frac{1}{n+1}(X_1^2 + \ldots + X_{g-1}^2 + X_N^2 + X_g^2 + \ldots + X_n^2) - \left(\frac{1}{n+1}(X_1 + \ldots + X_{g-1} + X_N + X_g + \ldots + X_n)\right)^2 \qquad (6.7)$$

New partial variances are calculated using expressions (6.6) and (6.7), and the new extremum located by inspection of all (n+1) results.

Perhaps the most noteworthy thing about these sensitivity tests is the large likelihood that the extreme values will not, in fact, be altered by inversion of rankings or by the introduction of a new state of nature. This is particularly so if it is assumed, in the former case, that the states inverted are unlikely, in general, to be very different in their initial ranking. The same is also true in the latter case, if it is assumed that any newly identified state of nature does not possess a very extreme payoff value and that it will stand a greater than average chance of being ranked low, on the grounds that otherwise it would have been recognised initially and included in the original ranking.

6.3 CHANGES IN PAYOFFS

In addition to the possibility of ranking changes, it is also of interest to assess the effect on extreme expected payoffs of strategies of possible changes in the individual payoffs. As previously, this will be undertaken by reference to a single strategy with payoffs $X_j (j=1...n)$. Although capable of extension, the analysis is most easily presented in terms of changes only of a single X_j value at any one time. It is quite likely that in a real decision problem, the X_j is but a rough estimate of the value of the outcome it represents, and as such it is important to discover what effect any estimation error may have on conclusions drawn about the extreme expected values.

It was shown in chapter 3 that the maximum and minimum expected payoffs of a strategy may be found by calculating a series of partial averages, starting with the payoff of the most likely state of nature and progressively adding the less likely ones. The largest partial average gives the maximum expected payoff and the smallest the minimum (see section 3.4). If the partial average for the jth state of nature is an optimum and this is indicated by an asterisk, i.e. $\bar{X}_{j*} = \frac{1}{j*} \sum_{k=1}^{j*} X_k$,

the following conditions must be satisfied:

$$\bar{X}_j - \bar{X}_{j*} \quad \begin{array}{l} (\leqslant 0 \quad \text{maximisation }) \\ (\geqslant 0 \quad \text{minimisation }) \end{array} \quad j = 1, 2....n ; j \neq j*$$

$$(6.8)$$

Suppose now that one of the strategy payoffs, X_p, is changed to $X_p + \delta$ where δ is a small constant. Clearly in order to ensure that the solution to the problem remains optimal, it is necessary to check whether the above conditions are still satisfied. Four separate cases may be identified for maximisation depending upon whether p is greater or less than j* and upon whether δ is positive or negative. Analogous results may be obtained for minimisation.

There will not be a change in the j*, if the following conditions are satisfied:

Maximisation

(1)   When δ is positive there are two possibilities:

   (a)   If $p \leqslant j^*$ it is only necessary to check that

$$\frac{1}{j}\left(\left(\sum_{k=1}^{j} X_k\right) + \delta\right) - \frac{1}{j^*}\left(\left(\sum_{k=1}^{j^*} X_k\right) + \delta\right) \leqslant 0 \text{ for } j = p, \dots j^*-1$$

which reduces to

$$\delta \leqslant \frac{j^* j}{j^* - j}\ (\bar{X}_{j^*} - \bar{X}_j) \text{ for } j = p, \dots j^*-1 \qquad (6.9)$$

Notice that partial averages $\bar{X}_1 \dots \bar{X}_{p-1}$ are unchanged and need not be considered, and partial averages $\bar{X}_{j^*+1}, \dots \bar{X}_n$ will be increased less than $\bar{X}_{j^*}$. Note too that if $p = j^*$, $\bar{X}_{j^*}$ remains maximal.

   (b)   When $p > j^*$ it is only necessary to check that

$$\frac{1}{j}\left(\left(\sum_{k=1}^{j} X_k\right) + \delta\right) - \frac{1}{j^*}\sum_{k=1}^{j^*} X_k \leqslant 0 \qquad\qquad \text{for } j = p, \dots n$$

which reduces to

$$\delta \leqslant j\ (\bar{X}_{j^*} - \bar{X}_j) \text{ for } j = p, \dots n \qquad (6.10)$$

Note that partial averages $\bar{X}_1, \dots \bar{X}_{p-1}$ are unchanged.

(2)   When δ is negative the maximum will not change if $p > j^*$. In this case only $\bar{X}_p, \dots \bar{X}_n$ will be reduced and $\bar{X}_{j^*}$ will remain maximal. If $p \leqslant j^*$ there are two possibilities:

   (a)   One of the unchanged partial averages, $\bar{X}_1, \dots \bar{X}_{p-1}$ might now become optimal. This will not be the case if the following condition is fulfilled:

$$\frac{1}{j}\sum_{k=1}^{j} X_k - \frac{1}{j^*}\left(\left(\sum_{k=1}^{j^*} X_k\right) + \delta\right) \leqslant 0 \qquad\qquad \text{for } j = 1, \dots p-1$$

which reduces to

$$\delta \geqslant j^*\ (\bar{X}_j - \bar{X}_{j^*}) \text{ for } j = 1, \dots p-1. \qquad (6.11)$$

Notice that there is no need to consider the partial averages $\bar{X}_p, \dots ,$ $\bar{X}_{j^*-1}$ because the reduction in the payoff X_p will reduce them more than $\bar{X}_{j^*}$.

   (b)   One of the partial averages $\bar{X}_{j^*+1}, \dots \bar{X}_n$ may now become larger than $\bar{X}_{j^*}$. This will not be the case if the following condition is fulfilled:

$$\frac{1}{j}\left(\left(\sum_{k=1}^{j} X_k\right) + \delta\right) - \frac{1}{j^*}\left(\left(\sum_{k=1}^{j^*} X_k\right) + \delta\right) \leqslant 0 \text{ for } j = j^*+1, \dots n$$

which reduces to

$$\delta \geqslant \frac{j j^*}{j - j^*}\ (\bar{X}_j - \bar{X}_{j^*}) \text{ for } j = j^*-1, \dots n. \qquad (6.12)$$

Both (6.11) and (6.12) must be checked to ensure that j* remains optimal.

Minimisation Conditions analogous to (6.9)...(6.12) are available for
              this situation.

(1)   When δ is negative there are two possibilities:
   (a)   When p < j*, it is only necessary to check that

$$\frac{1}{j} \left(\left(\sum_{k=1}^{j} X_k \right) + \delta \right) - \frac{1}{j*} \left(\left(\sum_{k=1}^{j*} X_k \right) + \delta \right) \geqslant 0 \qquad \text{for } j = p,... \ j-1$$

which reduces to

$$\delta \geqslant \frac{j*j}{j*-j} (\bar{X}_{j*} - \bar{X}_j) \qquad \text{for } j = p, ... \ j* - 1. \qquad (6.13)$$

Notice that result (6.13) is similar to (6.9), but the direction of the
inequality is reversed. Note too that if p = j*, $\bar{X}_{j*}$ remains minimal.

   (b)   When p > j*, it is only necessary to check that

$$\delta \geqslant j (\bar{X}_{j*} - \bar{X}_j) \qquad \text{for } j = p, ... \ n. \qquad (6.14)$$

The result is similar to (6.10), but the direction of the inequality is
reversed.

(2)   When δ is positive the minimum cannot change if p > j*. When
p $\leqslant$ j* there are two cases:

   (a) $\delta \leqslant j*(\bar{X}_j - \bar{X}_{j*})$ \qquad\qquad for j = 1, ... p - 1 \qquad (6.15)

   (b) $\delta \leqslant \frac{jj*}{j-j*} (\bar{X}_j - \bar{X}_{j*})$ \qquad for j = j*+1, ... n \qquad (6.16)

Conditions (6.15) and (6.16) must be fulfilled to ensure that j* remains
optimal.

   Note again that results (6.15) and (6.16) are similar to (6.11) and
(6.12) respectively, but the direction of the inequalities is reversed.

   The above conditions enable the optimality of any known solution to be
checked without having to recalculate all the partial averages should
there be a change in one of the strategy payoffs. If the change in
payoff is δ and if δ obeys the maximisation conditions, then the same set
of probabilities of states of nature will optimise the new problem which
gave the optimal solution to the original one. In this case the maximum
expected payoff changes from

$$\frac{1}{j*} \sum_{k=1}^{j*} X_k \qquad \text{to} \qquad \frac{1}{j*} \left(\sum_{k=1}^{j*} X_k \right) + \frac{1}{j*} \delta.$$

An exactly parallel argument holds for minimum expected payoff.

   Alternatively, the two sets of maximisation and minimisation
conditions can be used to delineate ranges of values for δ such that the
original extreme expected payoff probabilities do not change and so
provide a sensitivity test for the original solutions. Within the region

of δ changes located above, extreme expected values will always change by exactly $\frac{\delta}{j^*}$.

Finally, it may be observed that the effect of simultaneous changes in the payoffs in two or more states of nature may be examined in much the same way as has been just demonstrated. Parameters δ_1, δ_2, δ_3, etc. will have to be specified and more complex sets of minimisation and maximisation conditions obtained. The volume of algebra involved increases rapidly, although it is not intrinsically difficult.

An attempt has also been made to derive conditions similar to those given above for maximum variance. Unfortunately, it does not appear possible to obtain simple results.

6.4 SPECIFICATION OF RANGES FOR PAYOFFS

Another form of uncertainty about payoff values which might well be encountered in practice is the situation where individual X_j are not known with certainty, but are believed to lie in a range $X_{jL} \leqslant X_j \leqslant X_{jU}$. The extension of the original result on extreme expected values is quite straightforward in this case. It was shown in chapter 3 that for any given set of X_j for a single strategy, extreme expected values are found by calculating all partial averages,

$$\bar{X}_j = \frac{1}{j} \sum_{k=1}^{j} X_k, \qquad j = 1, \ldots n$$

and locating the minimum and maximum partial averages by inspection. Consider now

$$\frac{\partial \bar{X}_j}{\partial X_h} = \frac{1}{j} \qquad (1 \leqslant h \leqslant j).$$

Because the derivative is positive for all finite values of h and j, it can be asserted that increasing X_h will always increase $\bar{X}_j$ and conversely. Therefore, the highest $\bar{X}_j$ can only be attained by increasing all X_h (h = 1 .... j) to their upper limits, and conversely to obtain the lowest $\bar{X}_j$. Hence, maximum expected value may be located by applying the original partial averaging technique to all upper limits, X_{jU}, and minimum by applying it to all lower limits X_{jL}. This is completely in accord with intuition. An important point, however, is the ability to separate the location of the relevant X_j values from the identification of the optimal P_j sets. The X_j are set at their most extreme values first and then the optimal P_j are found by partial average calculations. This will be exploited also in seeking a maximum variance result.

To seek a constrained maximum for $\sum_{j=1}^{n} P_j (X_j - \bar{X})^2$ with P_j variable and and also X_j variable in the range $X_{jL} \leqslant X_j \leqslant X_{jU}$ is essentially a cubic non-linear programming problem and is not susceptible to analytical solution. However, a reasonably straightforward analytical result is possible, based on the recognition that, whatever the values of the X_j, the maximum variance will be found by locating the partial variance which is maximal. Hence, if each partial variance is maximised with respect to choice of X_j values within $X_{jL} \leqslant X_j \leqslant X_{jU}$, then the maximum of

these maxima will maximise the variance of payoffs. The problem, then,
is to determine whether there is any simple way of finding the maximum
of any general partial variance,

$$V_j = \frac{1}{j} \sum_{k=1}^{j} X_k^2 - (\frac{1}{j} \sum_{k=1}^{j} X_k)^2$$

Firstly, consider a two-dimensional illustration. Suppose as part of
a maximum variance calculation it is required to find the maximum
partial variance with exactly two possible payoffs, where the X_j are
constrained by $3 \leqslant X_1 \leqslant 5$ and $2 \leqslant X_2 \leqslant 4$. As shown in Figure 6.1, these
constraints give a square feasible region. Further, lines of constant
variance are 45^0 lines. From the diagram, V_2, the partial variance
with two states of nature included, is maximised when $X_1 = 5$ and $X_2 = 2$.

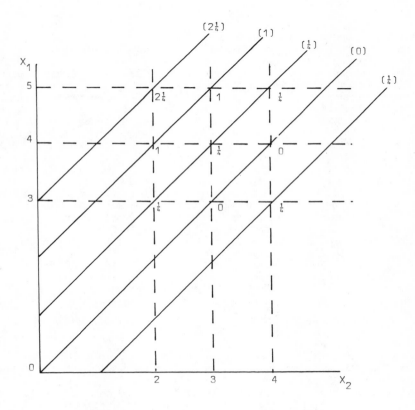

Figure 6.1 Variance Loci for a Two Variable Problem

It should be noted that variance is maximised at a corner point in the feasible region, that this corner point could never be (X_{1L}, X_{2L}) or (X_{1U}, X_{2U}) and that it is the corner perpendicularly furthest from the $45°, V = 0$ line. Unless the ranges of X_1 and X_2 are identical, there will always be a single variance-maximising corner point solution.

Returning now to the n variable problem, consider

$$\frac{\partial V_j}{\partial X_h} = \frac{2}{j} X_h - \frac{2}{j^2} \sum_{k=1}^{j} X_k$$

$$= \frac{2}{j} (X_h - \frac{1}{j} \sum_{k=1}^{j} X_k)$$

$$= \frac{2}{j} (X_h - \bar{X}_j) \qquad (1 \leqslant h \leqslant j)$$

The sign of this expression depends upon the bracketed term. It will be positive if X_h lies above the mean of all the X_k included in this particular partial variance calculation and conversely. This yields the intuitively acceptable result that, with all the other X_k held constant, variance can be increased by increasing X_h, if X_h lies above the mean, and by decreasing X_h, if X_h lies below the mean. Furthermore, the increase in variance will continue the more X_h is moved away from the mean. Hence, with all other X_k held constant, variance will be maximised by letting X_h take either its maximum or minimum value. But this argument may be repeated for all the X_h (h = 1 .... k). Whenever X_h is not at either its upper or lower bound value, variance can be increased by moving it towards the lower bound if X_h is already below the current partial average or towards the upper bound if X_h is above the current partial average. Hence it may be concluded that maximum partial variance for any j can be found by examining the 2^j possible partial variance figures corresponding to all combinations of X_{kU} and X_{kL} (k = 1 .... j). If the set of X_{kU} and X_{kL} which corresponds to a maximum is found for each value of j = 2 .... n, then the maximum possible variance for all values of P_j and X_j is simply the maximum of these maxima. The main problem which remains is the volume of computation, which grows exponentially with n. Although it will never be necessary to examine combinations which contain all upper bound or all lower bound X_j values, there appear to be no other a priori exclusions, which leaves a requirement of $\sum_{j=1}^{n} 2^j$ -2(n - 1) calculations.

6.5 CONCLUSIONS

It has been shown above that the results obtained in chapters 3 and 4 may be subjected to certain types of sensitivity analysis. This facility is particularly important given the doubts about available information which are bound to exist in many real applications of this decision making technique. These concern the accuracy of the ranking of probabilities of states of nature, the possible omission of relevant states of nature and the inaccuracy of the estimated payoffs. A number

of straightforward procedures were developed in this chapter to test the
sensitivity of the initial results to such changes. They provide the
decision maker with valuable tests of the robustness of this decision
making model and thus enhance its attractiveness.

7 Extension of the basic results: Bayesian estimation, probability matrix and entropy

7.1 INTRODUCTION

Three further aspects of decision making with ranked probabilities are explored in this chapter. It is shown in section 7.2 how the ranking of probabilities of future states of nature may be revised in a Bayesian fashion, to take account of experimental evidence in a situation when the states of nature remain unchanged in two or more decision problems. In section 7.3, the information available to the decision maker is restated in terms of outcomes and a probability matrix, rather than in terms of states of nature and a payoff matrix, and a new approach to decision making based on ranked, rather than precisely specified, probabilities is suggested. Section 7.4 deals with the use of entropy in decision making as described by Starr (1978), and discusses the implications of ranked probabilities for entropy.

7.2 EXPERIMENTAL EVIDENCE AND BAYESIAN REVISION OF RANKING

The main results of chapters 3 and 4 are based on the assumption that the decision maker is able to rank the probabilities of occurrence of future states of nature, i.e. $P_j \geq P_{j+1}$ where P_j is the probability of the jth state of nature and $j = 1, 2....(n-1)$. They show that maximum and minimum expected payoffs of a strategy can be obtained by calculating a series of partial averages, starting with the payoff of the most likely state of nature and progressively adding the less likely ones, see result (3.11). The largest partial average gives the maximum expected payoff of the strategy and the smallest the minimum. Similarly, the maximum and minimum variances of the strategy can be obtained by calculating a series of partial variances, starting with the payoff of the most likely state of nature and progressively adding the less likely ones. The maximum variance is given by the largest partial variance while the minimum variance is always zero. A combination of limiting expected payoffs and maximum variance (or standard deviation) was used in chapter 5 as a criterion for strategy selection.

Now imagine a decision maker facing a small number of sequential decision problems whose states of nature and their probabilities remain the same from one decision problem to another. Due to lack of perfect foresight, however, he does not know the exact values of the probabilities, but has enough information to be able to rank them. Finding himself in this situation, he would be unwise to approach successive decision problems as if the outcomes of the previous ones had no bearing on them. It is obviously preferable to utilise the information obtained in previous trials to check whether the initial probability ranking is consistent with it. If the ranking is adjusted, more reliable limiting expected payoffs and variances will, in general, be obtained, and can be utilised in the following decision problems. The revision of the ranking of probabilities can be attempted on Bayesian lines.

The fundamental assumption, underlying the results obtained in chapters 3 and 4 concerns the decision maker's ability to rank the probabilities of the states of nature. In order to do this, he must consider all the n! possible rankings open to him, and select the one which, in his opinion, is most likely to be the correct one. If a collective body, e.g. a panel of experts, is the decision maker, the selection of the most likely ranking may be obtained by a voting procedure. By admitting the possibility of more than one ranking, the range of possible probabilities, which is associated with any one state of nature, is increased.

For example, suppose a manufacturer experiences an increase in demand for his products and decides to buy a basic raw material from a new supplier. The quality of the raw material can be of type A (good), B (fair), or C (poor) and is not known to the manufacturer. The raw material can be used in three processes in which the profit or loss to the manufacturer depends on the quality of the input used. There are no facilities to test the quality before its use. The manufacturer has to decide in which of the three processes he should use the newly purchased raw material.

In this decision problem there are three states of nature corresponding to the different qualities of the raw material. The manufacturer is unable to specify exactly the probabilities of the various states of nature but he has enough information about the new supplier to be able to rank them. He also estimates the probability of the most likely ranking, as well as the probabilities of the other possible ranking hypotheses:

		Probability
H_1 :	$P_A \geqslant P_B \geqslant P_C$	0.30
H_2 :	$P_A \geqslant P_C \geqslant P_B$	0.20
H_3 :	$P_B \geqslant P_A \geqslant P_C$	0.25
H_4 :	$P_B \geqslant P_C \geqslant P_A$	0.10
H_5 :	$P_C \geqslant P_A \geqslant P_B$	0.10
H_6 :	$P_C \geqslant P_B \geqslant P_A$	0.05

Previously, H_1, the hypothesis with the highest probability, would have been chosen and the others largely ignored. The sensitivity tests discussed in chapter 6 enable consideration of other hypotheses, but not all hypotheses would normally be investigated. If H_1 is selected, the minimum probability of A is fixed as $1/3$; if all hypotheses are considered, the minimum value of P_A can be zero if subsequent evidence suggests that this is likely. Thus, the full range of values, $0 \leqslant P_A \leqslant 1$, becomes effective.

The ranking specified under H_1 is normally used in the initial calculation of the limiting expected payoffs and variances. Suppose, however, that the results of the first purchase indicate that state of nature B has occurred, i.e. that the quality of the material is only fair. Then a Bayesian approach may be used to revise the probabilities associated with each of the six ranking hypotheses. This requires the assumption that, if B has occurred, then the actual probability of B was the maximum consistent with each ranking hypothesis. This is essentially a 'conservative' assumption aiming to ensure that the initial probabilities of the six hypotheses are changed as little as possible in the light of the experimental evidence. Given this assumption it is possible to calculate the probability that H_1 is the correct hypothesis, given that the state of nature B has occurred, using Bayes theorem:

$$P(H_1 \mid B) = \frac{P(H_1)P(B \mid H_1)}{\sum_{i=1}^{6} P(H_i)P(B \mid H_i)} = \frac{0.3 \times 0.5}{0.3 \times 0.5 + 0.2 \times 0.33 + \ldots} = 0.24 \text{ approx.}$$

Note that the maximum value of P_B under H_1 is $1/2$, under H_2, $1/3$, under H_3, 1, etc. Similarly, $P(H_2 \mid B) = 0.106$, $P(H_3 \mid B) = 0.401$, $P(H_4 \mid B) = 0.160$, $P(H_5 \mid B) = 0.053$ and $P(H_6 \mid B) = 0.040$; $\sum_{i=1}^{6} P(H_i \mid B) = 1$ as required.

Thus, in this situation, the probability ranking of the hypotheses has changed. H_3 is now the most likely hypothesis, and, therefore, in the next decision problem the ranking $P_B \geqslant P_A \geqslant P_C$ should be used for selecting a strategy. Clearly, depending upon the payoffs of the strategies under assessment, it is possible that a different strategy will be chosen with the H_3 ranking than with the H_1. When the result of the second outcome becomes available, the new probabilities can be revised again.

It is also worth noting that the minimum value of $P(B \mid H_i) = 0$ for i = 1, 2, 5, 6 and $1/3$ for i = 3, 4 and, therefore, the least 'conservative' estimate of $P(H_i \mid B) = 0$ for i = 1, 2, 5, 6 while

$$P(H_3 \mid B) = \frac{0.25 \times 0.33}{0.25 \times 0.33 + 0.10 \times 0.33} = 0.71 \text{ approx}$$

and $P(H_4 \mid B) = 0.29$ approx. This extreme revision of probabilities in the light of one outcome is obviously undesirable, because it is unrealistic to assume that $P(H_i \mid B) = 0$ for i = 1, 2, 5, 6. However, it would be possible to average the most 'conservative' and the least 'conservative' estimates to obtain intermediate values.

The inclusion of the possibility of changing the most likely ranking order of the probabilities of the states of nature in the light of experimental evidence, increases the flexibility of the decision making model presented in chapters 3, 4 and 5, and, hence, should improve the quality of decision making resulting from its use.

7.3   OUTCOMES AND THE PROBABILITY MATRIX

It was assumed in chapter 3 that the decision maker is able to specify strategies S_i (i = 1, 2....m) open to him, the states of nature N_j (j = 1, 2....n), under which these strategies may have to operate and the payoffs X_{ij} corresponding to the various combinations of strategies and states of nature. There the X_{ij} payoff was a function of the ith strategy and the jth state of nature, i.e. $X_{ij} = f(S_i, N_j)$. It is probably more realistic to assume, as is done in section 6.3, that X_{ij} is a stochastic variable, rather than a uniquely determined single value. Such an assumption simply reflects the fact that there are many factors involved in the evaluation of a payoff, and that some of them are not known precisely, e.g. estimation of net present value of an investment.

Starr (1978) uses the payoff matrix approach outlined above, but he also suggests that in many situations the decision maker is unable to specify all the relevant states of nature and the payoffs associated with them, and that this constitutes an additional source of uncertainty for him. The difficulty may be due to the fact that he does not possess enough information to evaluate precisely the payoffs for the relevant states of nature, or that there are so many relevant states of nature, (e.g. when they relate to the timing of an upturn in the economy), that it is impracticable to evaluate their payoffs. Faced with this situation, the decision maker is well advised to reformulate his problem along the lines suggested by Starr (1978). This involves enumeration of a number of outcomes (equivalent to payoffs in the other formulation) which in his view are likely to arise if he adopts a particular strategy. Unlike the payoffs, the outcomes are not related to specific states of nature. If O_1 is the minimum outcome specified for all strategies and O_r the maximum, $O_{ih} = f(S_i)$, where $h = 1, 2....r$, i.e. the hth outcome of the ith strategy depends only on the strategy and not on a specific state of nature. There may in fact, be many states of nature which can produce the outcome O_{ih} but they are not generally known. Starr assumes further, that the decision maker is able to assign subjective probabilities to these outcomes. Thus it is possible to construct a matrix with strategies S_i, $i = 1, 2....m$, represented by rows, outcomes O_h, $h = 1, 2....r$, by columns and with P_{ih} as elements where $\sum_{h=1}^{r} P_{ih} = 1$ for all i by definition, i.e. the outcomes are assumed to be exhaustive and mutually exclusive. Many of the probabilities will often be zero, as some outcomes will be impossible under some strategies.

An important advantage of the reformulation of the problem in terms of outcomes is that it is still possible to calculate expected values and variances for strategies, in spite of the fact that the exact specification of states of nature is no longer assumed. It is also possible to allow the originally used payoffs, X_{ij}, to behave as random variables, i.e. if X_{ij} is a central estimate, X_{ijU} an upper estimate and X_{ijL} a lower estimate of the payoff, the probability P_j can be partitioned between the three estimates and each of them can be treated as a separate outcome. Moreover, the new formulation enables the use of the criterion of statistical dominance in strategy selection (see Starr (1978) section 5.1) and makes possible the evaluation of entropy, which can be used as an indication of the degree of uncertainty associated with a probability distribution (see Starr (1978) section 5.3 and section 7.4 below).

The most unrealistic assumption made in the reformulation of the problem concerns the specification of exact probabilities of outcomes. It is argued in chapter 3 that even when the relevant states of nature can be readily identified, it is unreasonable to expect the decision maker to be able to specify the probabilities. The same considerations suggest that it is even more unlikely that he can specify exactly the probabilities of outcomes. The nature of the reformulation of the problem in terms of outcomes makes it clear that the specification of the exact probabilities of outcomes is more difficult than the specification of probabilities of states of nature. This is because the decision maker is now expected to know the probability of a particular outcome, although he may not know which state (or states) of nature generate the outcome, nor the probability of occurrence of the state (or states) of nature.

The above considerations suggest that it would be more realistic to make a less stringent assumption about the probabilities of outcomes. If it is assumed, for example, that the decision maker can only rank the probabilities of outcomes, it is possible to evaluate the minimum and maximum expected values of outcomes and their minimum and maximum variances using results (3.11) and (4.9). In order to obtain the limiting expected outcomes of a strategy, it is necessary to calculate a series of partial averages, starting with the most likely outcome and progressively adding less likely ones. A typical partial average for the ith strategy is given by $\frac{1}{h} \sum_{k=1}^{h} 0_{ik}$, where h = 1, 2....r. (This

means, of course, that the order in which the outcomes are introduced is in general different from the order in which they are listed above the columns of the probability matrix). The smallest partial average gives the minimum expected outcome and the largest the maximum. Minimum and maximum variances are obtained in an analogous way, by calculating a series of partial variances, starting with the most likely outcomes and progressively adding less likely ones. A typical partial variance for the ith strategy is given by:

$$\frac{1}{h} \sum_{k=1}^{h} 0_{ik}^2 - (\frac{1}{h} \sum_{k=1}^{h} 0_{ik})^2$$

where again h = 1, 2....r. Minimum variance of a strategy is always zero, but the maximum differs between strategies and is given by the largest partial variance.

The final selection of a strategy may be based on minimum or maximum expected value or some combination of the two. This problem is discussed in some detail in chapter 3. Maximum variance (or maximum standard deviation) can be used as an additional decision making criterion. Large variance is usually regarded as undesirable, for it implies greater 'inaccuracy' in the expected outcome and, therefore, in many circumstances, it may be necessary to trade off expected value against variance. This problem is also discussed in chapters 4 and 5.(1)

7.4 ENTROPY

The aim of this section is to comment on the use of entropy in decision making and to explore its implications for ranked probabilities as used in chapters 3 and 4.

A well known method of evaluating the uncertainty associated with a probability distribution is to calculate its entropy. It can be computed for the probability distribution applicable to the states of nature of the payoff matrix, referred to in section 7.3 and is defined as: $E = -\sum_{j=1}^{n} P_j \log_2 P_j$

where j = 1, 2....n, P_j is the probability of occurrence of the jth
state of nature and $\sum_{j=1}^{n} P_j = 1$. It can also be calculated for the
probability distributions of individual strategies which appear as rows
of the probability matrix when the problem is reformulated in terms of
outcomes. In this case entropy is defined as:

$$E = - \sum_{h=1}^{r} P_h \log_2 P_h$$

where h = 1, 2....r, P_h is the probability of the hth outcome and
$\sum_{h=1}^{r} P_h = 1$.

   In addition to expected value and variance, Starr (1978) pp. 32-33
uses entropy as a further criterion for assessing attractiveness of
strategies. It does not depend on the payoffs or outcomes, and,
therefore, differs fundamentally from the other measures. It varies
between zero and $\log_2 n$ (or $\log_2 r$) and indicates the degree of uncertainty
underlying a probability distribution. The maximum uncertainty (and
maximum entropy) occurs when all states of nature (or outcomes) are
equally likely, i.e. when $P_j = 1/n$ for all j (or $P_h = 1/r$ for all h).
This situation corresponds to decision making under uncertainty when the
criterion of 'insufficient reason' is invoked. In such a case, the
decision maker is assumed to have no information about the probabilities
and, therefore, assumes that they are all equal. As soon as he is able
to differentiate between the probabilities, entropy falls, indicating
that the new situation is less uncertain. When one state of nature (or
outcome) is certain to occur its probability is equal to one, while the
other probabilities are all zero. Then entropy is zero, indicating that
there is no uncertainty about the future. Entropy also depends on the
number of states of nature (or outcomes), e.g. maximum entropy is given
by $\log_2 n$ (or $\log_2 r$) and, therefore, the larger n (or r) is, the larger
the entropy.

   Starr (1978) section 5.3 first calculates entropy for the probability
distribution of the states of nature of a hypothetical decision problem
with two strategies, then reformulates it in terms of outcomes and
calculates entropies for the probability distributions of the outcomes
of the two strategies. The first two values of entropy are higher than
the second two, suggesting that the decision making environment is more
uncertain when states of nature are available than when only outcomes
are identified. This implication is obviously unexpected and worrying.
Starr concludes that the illustration leads to the general counter-
intuitive conclusion that: 'while the decision (payoff) matrix provides
more information than the outcome (probability) matrix, it also creates
greater uncertainty'. This apparent paradox, which implies that either
intuition is misleading or entropy is not a very satisfactory measure of
uncertainty, can, however, be resolved in a way which suggests that there
is nothing wrong with either intuition or entropy.

   The difficulty arises in Starr's example because two payoffs of each
strategy repeat themselves. Thus when the problem is reformulated in
terms of outcomes, the number of outcomes is smaller than the number of
payoffs, and therefore, a decline in entropy is observed. It is possible
to argue however, that when payoffs of a strategy repeat themselves

(which is not very likely in practice), their states of nature (and their probabilities) should be combined. Distinguishing between these states of nature does not produce any additional information about the probabilities of payoffs or outcomes. If this is done, the payoffs and outcomes of a strategy, and their probability distributions, are identical, and, therefore, their entropies are equal too. Such a result is in agreement with expectations, indicating that the degree of uncertainty in the reformulated problem can never be less than in the original one. Thus there is little point in comparing situations, like the ones discussed by Starr, with respect to entropy. The ability to link payoffs to states of nature, however, does provide the decision maker with additional information, but this is not measured by entropy. When outcomes cannot be related to the states of nature which generate them, entropy is a useful measure of uncertainty underlying the probability distributions of strategies.

It is also interesting to look at the assumptions about probabilities of states of nature made in chapters 3 and 4, and to evaluate their implications for entropy. It was assumed there that the decision maker can rank the probabilities, i.e. $P_j \geqslant P_{j+1}$, $j = 1,2....(n-1)$. In these circumstances, maximum entropy arises when $P_j = 1/n$ for all j, and is equal to $\log_2 n$. Minimum entropy is zero and occurs when $P_1 = 1$ while all the other probabilities are equal to zero. As the two probability distributions producing extreme values of entropy satisfy the ranking constraint, its introduction does not affect the range of entropy. This must not be taken to imply that the introduction of ranking does not affect uncertainty about the future. Many probability distributions, e.g. all those were $P_{j+1} > P_j$, are eliminated by ranking and, therefore, considerable reduction in the uncertainty about the future occurs, but the entropies of the remaining ones still cover the full range from 0 to $\log_2 n$. This suggests that entropy is not an ideal measure of the uncertainty underlying a probability distribution.

In chapter 3 it was shown that the imposition of the ranking constraint produces a range for expected payoff which is, in general, considerably smaller than the range of payoffs. This result provides useful additional information to the decision maker, yet the range of entropy is unaffected by ranking, implying that the uncertainty about the future is unchanged. This property must reduce the usefulness of entropy in decision making. It highlights the rather narrow conception of uncertainty implicit in the entropy measure.

Finally, there is the problem of trade-off between expected value, variance (or standard deviation) and entropy. It was mentioned above that entropy can be useful when the decision problem is formulated in terms of outcomes and a probability matrix. The question immediately arises as to what importance should the decision maker attach to entropy as compared with the other two indicators. Most decision makers are familiar with basic statistical concepts like expected value and variance (or standard deviation), but are likely to be unfamiliar with the rather complex concept of entropy. Some general guidance may, therefore, be helpful.

It should be remembered that, unlike expected value and variance (or standard deviation), entropy is independent of payoffs or outcomes, and, therefore, on its own is less useful than the other measures. It is, in general, independent of expected value, i.e. small values of entropy do not imply small expected payoffs, nor do large values of entropy imply large expected payoffs. It is, however, slightly related to variance (or standard deviation) because, ceteris paribus, both measures tend to increase as the number of payoffs, or outcomes, increases. The relationship need not be very strong, and can be very weak. In most situations, expected value is likely to be the most important indicator in decision making, followed by variance (or standard deviation). Entropy is probably less important than variance (or standard deviation), and should generally be used only when the other two measures fail to distinguish decisively between competing strategies.

7.5   CONCLUSIONS

It was shown above that the results obtained in chapters 3, 4 and 5 can be extended to deal with a number of problems met in decision making. Sequential revision of probability ranking of states of nature is useful when a decision is taken more than once in conditions in which states of nature and their probabilities do not change. The results were also used to calculate extreme expected outcomes and variances in a situation when it was impossible, or impracticable, to relate outcomes to states of nature, and when it was unreasonable to assume that exact probabilities of outcomes were available. It was also shown that the use of entropy as a measure of the degree of uncertainty in a probability distribution of outcomes is not very satisfactory because the imposition of the ranking constraint on the probabilities does not affect the range of entropy.(2) Finally it was argued that entropy is less useful in decision making than extreme expected values and maximum variance of outcomes.

NOTES

(1) It is also worth noting that if the decision maker can specify a strict ranking of probabilities of outcomes, he can use result (3.16) to calculate maximum and minimum expected outcomes of strategies.

(2) If strict ranking of probabilities is applicable, maximum entropy will, in general, be less than $\log_2 n$ (or $\log_2 r$) and the minimum greater than zero.

8 Weak dominance

8.1 INTRODUCTION

The aim of this chapter is to propose a new criterion of weak statistical
dominance of one strategy over another and to explore its implications.
The criterion is defined in section 8.2 and its relationship to strict
statistical dominance is established. The interpretation of the new
concept is discussed in section 8.3 which also suggests possible uses
of the new criterion in decision making. The relationship between weak
dominance in terms of payoffs and regret, as traditionally defined, is
investigated in section 8.4 and it is shown that weak dominance in terms
of payoffs is equivalent to weak dominance in terms of regret. Numerical
examples are presented in section 8.5 to illustrate the theoretical
results obtained in the earlier sections. Concluding remarks are made
in section 8.6.

8.2 DEFINITION OF WEAK STATISTICAL DOMINANCE

It was pointed out in chapter 3 that the demanding conditions required
for Fishburn's strict dominance (see section 3.2) are unlikely to be
fulfilled in most realistic decision problems. It was for this reason
that a new approach to decision making was developed in chapters 3, 4
and 5 based on maximum and minimum expected payoffs and maximum variance
of strategies. It may be argued, however, that a sole reliance on
limiting expected payoffs of strategies is undesirable. A more direct
comparison of corresponding payoffs of two strategies has certain
advantages. This can be done by looking at the extreme values of the
difference between expected payoffs of two strategies, i.e. $E(S_1)-E(S_2)$
or

$$\Sigma P_j X_{1j} - \Sigma P_j X_{2j} = \Sigma P_j (X_{1j} - X_{2j}) = \Sigma P_j D_j \qquad (j = 1, 2....n) \ (8.1)$$

where $D_j = (X_{1j} - X_{2j})$ is the difference between corresponding payoffs
of strategies S_1 and S_2 for the jth state of nature. In fact, result
(8.1) defines the expected value of the differences.

Assuming the ranking constraint still holds, i.e. $P_j \geq P_{j+1}$, for
$j = 1, 2....(n-1)$, it is possible to find maximum and minimum $\{E(S_1)-E(S_2)\}$
and these may be compared with maximum and minimum $\{E(S_2)-E(S_1)\}$. The
results obtained in chapter 3 are directly applicable here. They show
that maximum and minimum expected differences can be found by simply
evaluating partial averages of the differences:

$$\bar{D}_j = \frac{1}{j} \sum_{k=1}^{j} D_k , \qquad (j = 1, 2....n) \ (8.2)$$

The largest of these is the maximum expected difference and the smallest
the minimum.

If the situation is viewed from the standpoint of strategy 2, the quantity of interest is:

$$\{E(S_2) - E(S_1)\} = \Sigma P_j D_j' \qquad (j = 1, 2 .... n) \qquad (8.3)$$

where $D_j' = (X_{2j} - X_{1j})$. Maximum and minimum $\{E(S_2) - E(S_1)\}$ can be found using result (8.2) by replacing D_j by D_j'. In fact this is not necessary because $D_j = -D_j'$ and, therefore, $\bar{D}_j = -\bar{D}_j'$ and it follows immediately that

$$\max\{E(S_2) - E(S_1)\} = -\min\{E(S_1) - E(S_2)\}$$

and $\qquad\qquad\qquad\qquad\qquad\qquad\qquad\qquad\qquad\qquad$ (8.4)

$$\min\{E(S_2) - E(S_1)\} = -\max\{E(S_1) - E(S_2)\}$$

Thus the four limiting values can be obtained from result (8.2). The largest $\bar{D}_j$ gives $\max\{E(S_1) - E(S_2)\}$ and when its sign is changed it becomes $\min\{E(S_2) - E(S_1)\}$. The smallest $\bar{D}_j$ gives $\min\{E(S_1) - E(S_2)\}$ and when its sign is changed it becomes $\max\{E(S_2) - E(S_1)\}$.

It also follows from result (8.4) that

if $\qquad\quad \max\{E(S_1) - E(S_2)\} > \max\{E(S_2) - E(S_1)\}$

then $\qquad \min\{E(S_1) - E(S_2)\} > \min\{E(S_2) - E(S_1)\}$.

Thus when

$$\max\{E(S_1) - E(S_2)\} > \max\{E(S_2) - E(S_1)\} \qquad (8.5)$$

it can be said that strategy 1 dominates weakly strategy 2. The term weak dominance is used here to distinguish it from Fishburn's strict dominance described in section 3.2.

Special case In fact strict dominance is a special case of the more general concept of weak dominance. When result (8.5) holds, S_1 dominates weakly S_2, and when additionally

$$\min\{E(S_1) - E(S_2)\} > 0,$$

S_1 dominates S_2 strictly in the Fishburn sense. The result follows immediately from equation (8.2) and the rule for locating the minimum.

$$\min\{E(S_1) - E(S_2)\} > 0$$

when

$$\bar{D}_j > 0 \qquad \text{for } j = 1, 2 .... n$$

i.e. when

$$\frac{1}{j} \{(X_{11} - X_{21}) + (X_{12} - X_{22}) + \cdots \cdots + (X_{1j} - X_{2j})\} > 0,$$

$$\text{for } j = 1, 2 .... n,$$

but this reduces to

$$(X_{11}+X_{12}+\ldots+X_{1j}) > (X_{21}+X_{22}+\ldots+X_{2j}), \text{ for } j = 1,2\ldots n,$$

$$(8.6)$$

which gives the conditions for strict dominance, see result (3.3) in chapter 3. Thus, when weak dominance is investigated it is only necessary to check that all $\bar{D}_j$ are positive to establish strict dominance.

8.3 INTERPRETATION AND POSSIBLE USES OF THE WEAK DOMINANCE CRITERION

Focusing on the differences between corresponding payoffs of strategies is quite common in decision theory. It is similar to defining regret in a decision problem with only two strategies (see section 2.4), but there is one important difference. Regret, as commonly used in decision theory, can only be positive or zero, e.g. if $X_{1j} \geqslant X_{2j}$, regret for S_1 and N_j is zero, and if $X_{1j} < X_{2j}$, it is equal to $(X_{2j} - X_{1j})$. Differences between corresponding payoffs, on the other hand, can be positive or negative. This is equivalent to allowing negative regret, which implies that the decision maker derives satisfaction when the payoff of a selected strategy is larger than the corresponding payoff of the rejected one. Such a view seems appropriate when making a direct comparison between two strategies and implies that differences between payoffs are preferable to regret for such a purpose. A further connection between differences and regret is discussed in section 8.4.

When weak dominance of S_1 over S_2 is established, it shows that, given the ranking constraint, the probability distribution most favourable to S_1 gives a maximum expected difference which is larger than the maximum expected difference (defined with respect to S_2) given by the probability distribution most favourable to S_2. A similar relationship obtains for the minima of the two expected differences, i.e. the minimum expected difference, calculated from the standpoint of S_1, is larger than the minimum expected difference calculated from the standpoint of S_2. If S_1 dominates S_2 weakly, but not strictly, there must exist probability distributions which satisfy the ranking constraint, but which ensure that $E(S_2) > E(S_1)$. This explains the weak aspect of the concept of dominance proposed in section 8.2.

The weak dominance criterion can be readily employed in a situation in which the original decision problem is reduced to the choice of one strategy from two competing ones. In this case focusing on the merits of one strategy relative to the other seems particularly pertinent. The criterion can also be used to eliminate similar strategies in a preliminary assessment of the decision problem. If two strategies out of a larger number differ only in minor details, but neither strictly dominates the other, it is possible to use the weak dominance criterion to eliminate one of them from further consideration.

Use of the weak dominance criterion in a decision problem containing more than two strategies is more complex. This is due to the fact that it lacks the property of transitivity among strategies, i.e. if S_1 dominates S_2 and S_2 dominates S_3, it does not necessarily follow that

74

S_1 dominates S_3. In such a situation it will be difficult to employ the criterion unless some measure of the strength of dominance is devised. An attempt at doing this is described in section 8.5. In many decision problems weak dominance will be transitive and then the criterion can be used (perhaps in conjunction with others) to select a strategy from among a larger number of competing ones. It must be remembered, however, that to establish transitivity, it is necessary to compare all strategies in pairs, i.e. if there are m strategies $\frac{1}{2}m(m-1)$ comparisons need to be made.

In spite of obvious similarities the results obtained in section 8.2 differ significantly from those obtained in section 3.3. For instance, it might be thought that

$$\max \{E(S_1) - E(S_2)\} = \max E(S_1) - \min E(S_2) \qquad (8.7)$$

This is not generally the case. Looking at strengths and weaknesses of one strategy in relation to another is rather different from looking at strategies in isolation. For the same reason it is not generally true that

if $\qquad \max E(S_1) > \max E(S_2)$ $\qquad\qquad\qquad\qquad\qquad\qquad (8.8)$

then $\qquad \max \{E(S_1) - E(S_2)\} > \max \{E(S_2) - E(S_1)\}$.

i.e. if maximum expected payoff of S_1 is larger than maximum expected payoff of S_2, it does not follow that S_1 dominates weakly S_2.

8.4 WEAK DOMINANCE AND REGRET

It is interesting to note that weak dominance in terms of payoffs is equivalent to weak dominance in terms of regret as defined in section 2.4. For this purpose it does not matter if there are two or more strategies in a decision problem. This relationship underlines further the similarities between differences between corresponding payoffs and regret.

In order to show this, consider a general decision problem with strategies S_i, i = 1, 2....m, states of nature N_j, j = 1, 2....n, payoffs X_{ij} and maximum payoffs for states of nature M_j, j = 1, 2....n. The element of the regret matrix corresponding to the X_{ij} payoff in the payoff matrix is given by $R_{ij} = M_j - X_{ij}$. For any two strategies, say 1 and 2, the difference between two regrets for the jth state of nature is given by

$$R_{1j} - R_{2j} = (M_j - X_{1j}) - (M_j - X_{2j}) = -(X_{1j} - X_{2j}) = -D_j$$

where D_j is the difference between payoffs as defined in equation (8.1) and (8.2). Therefore, it follows immediately from results (8.3) and (8.4) that

$\qquad\qquad \max \{E(S_1) - E(S_2)\} = -\min \{E(S_1) - E(S_2)\}$
$\qquad\qquad$ (in terms of payoffs) $\qquad$ (in terms of regret)

and

$\qquad\qquad \min \{E(S_1) - E(S_2)\} = -\max \{E(S_1) - E(S_2)\} \qquad (8.9)$
$\qquad\qquad$ (in terms of payoffs) $\qquad$ (in terms of regret)

It can be inferred from result (8.9) that if S_1 dominates weakly S_2 in terms of payoffs, i.e. when

$$\max \{E(S_1) - E(S_2) \} > \max \{E(S_2) - E(S_1)\}$$

it follows that S_1 also dominates weakly S_2 in terms of regrets, i.e.

$$\max \{E(S_1) - E(S_2)\} < \max \{ E(S_2) - E(S_1)\}.$$

It should be remembered that when regret is used the aim of the decision maker is to select the strategy which gives the lower expected difference between corresponding regrets of two competing strategies. Thus when weak dominance in terms of payoffs is established, it also establishes weak dominance in terms of regret. This relationship increases the usefulness of the weak dominance criterion for decision making.

8.5 NUMERICAL EXAMPLES

As an illustration of the results obtained in sections 8.2, 8.3 and 8.4 consider a decision problem faced by a branch manager of a large retail shop. He is offered two new products by the company sales manager, of which he has to choose one, i.e. S_1 = select product 1 and S_2 = select product 2. He distinguishes three states of nature which will affect sales prospects of the products in the immediate future: N_1 = no change, N_2 = improvement and N_3 = deterioration in economic conditions. The exact probabilities of the states of nature are not known to him but he believes that $P_1 \geqslant P_2 \geqslant P_3$. Profits (in £'000) for different combinations of strategies and states of nature are given in the body of the payoff matrix shown in Figure 8.1.

Strategy	State of Nature		
	N_1	N_2	N_3
S_1	3	12	4
S_2	8	2	-7

Figure 8.1 Payoff Matrix for the First Numerical Example

The decision maker knows that other branch managers have to make similar choices and that his performance will be assessed by the company's sales manager in relation to results of other branch managers. In these circumstances the evaluation of the merits of one strategy in isolation is less desirable than its assessment in relation to the other strategy which may be adopted by other branch managers. These are the conditions in which the criterion of weak dominance is particularly useful.

Using result (8.6) we first check that neither strategy strictly dominates the other, which here is the case since $3 < 8$, but $(3 + 12) > (8 + 2)$. In order to establish weak dominance it is necessary to compute differences between corresponding payoffs: $D_1 = 3 - 8 = -5$, $D_2 = 12 - 2 = 10$, and $D_3 = 4 + 7 = 11$. Using result (8.2) the partial averages of the differences are: $\bar{D}_1 = (-5)/1 = -5$, $\bar{D}_2 = (-5+10)/2 = 2\frac{1}{2}$ and $\bar{D}_3 = (-5 + 10 + 11)/3 = 5^1/_3$, and it follows from result (8.3) that $\max \{E(S_1) - E(S_2)\} = 5^1/_3$ and $\min \{E(S_1) - E(S_2)\} = -5$. Using result (8.4) we also have: $\max \{E(S_2) - E(S_1)\} = 5$ and $\min \{E(S_2) - E(S_1)\} = -5^1/_3$. Since $5^1/_3 > 5$, we deduce from result (8.5) that S_1 has a slight

weak dominance over S_2. This appears to be consistent with a quick
appraisal of the strategies. S_2 does better than S_1 under N_1, the
most likely state of nature, but under the two less likely states of
nature N_2 and N_3, S_1 is considerably more attractive than S_2. The weak
dominance criterion balances the two effects taking into account the
ranked probabilities of the states of nature and the differences between
payoffs. Weak dominance of S_1 over S_2 suggests that the branch manager
should select product 1 in preference to product 2 if he wants to compare
well with a branch manager who selects product 2. This does not mean, of
course, that S_1 will always perform better than S_2, e.g. under state of
nature N_1, S_2 is preferable to S_1, but assuming the branch manager uses
the weak dominance criterion to make a large number of similar decisions,
he will do better in the long run than his competitor who does not employ
the criterion.

The above example can also be used to show that, in general, results
(8.7) and (8.8) do not hold. Applying result (8.2) to payoffs of S_1
(rather than the differences) gives the following partial averages:
$\bar{X}_1 = 3$, $\bar{X}_2 = (3 + 12)/2 = 7\frac{1}{2}$ and $\bar{X}_3 = (3 + 12 + 4)/3 = 6^1/3$, and,
therefore, max $E(S_1) = 7\frac{1}{2}$ and min $E(S_1) = 3$. Analogous results for S_2
are: $\bar{X}_1 = 8$, $\bar{X}_2 = 5$ and $\bar{X}_3 = 1$ and, therefore, max $E(S_2) = 8$ and
min $E(S_2) = 1$. As max $\{E(S_1) - E(S_2)\} = 5^1/3$ does not equal max $E(S_1)$ -
min $E(S_2) = 7\frac{1}{2} - 1 = 6\frac{1}{2}$, result (8.7) is verified. Moreover, max $E(S_2)$
= 8 is larger than max $E(S_1) = 7\frac{1}{2}$ but S_1 dominates weakly S_2 as
max $\{E(S_1) - E(S_2)\} = 5^1/3$ is larger than max $\{E(S_2) - E(S_1)\} = 5$, which
verifies result (8.8).

As an illustration of the non-transitivity of the weak dominance
criterion among strategies, discussed in section 8.3, consider the
following decision problem where the states of nature are the same as
in Figure 8.1 and the branch manager has to select one new product out
of three offered to him by the company sales manager. The payoffs for
the various combinations of states of nature and strategies are shown in
the body of Figure 8.2.

Strategy	State of Nature		
	N_1	N_2	N_3
S_1	8	2	7
S_2	0	12	-3
S_3	3	-3	21

Figure 8.2 Payoff Matrix for the Second Numerical Example

Applying result (8.2) successively to all pairs of strategies, i.e.
$m(m-1)/2 = (3 \times 2)/2 = 3$, gives: max $\{E(S_1) - E(S_2)\} = 8$, while
max $\{E(S_2) - E(S_1)\} = 2$, therefore, S_1 dominates weakly S_2;
max $\{E(S_2) - E(S_3)\} = 6$, while max $\{E(S_3) - E(S_2)\} = 4$, therefore S_2
dominates weakly S_3; max $\{E(S_1) - E(S_3)\} = 5$ while max $\{E(S_3) - E(S_1)\} = 6$,
and therefore, S_3 dominates weakly S_1. Thus, if S_1 dominates weakly
S_2, and S_2 dominates weakly S_3, it does not necessarily follow that S_1
dominates weakly S_3. Because of the lack of transitivity, the branch
manager has a difficult choice to make. He should probably choose S_1,
as it dominates S_2 convincingly, while S_2 dominates S_3 less decisively,
and the dominance of S_3 over S_1 is very marginal, i.e. the difference

between max $\{E(S_1) - E(S_2)\}$ and max $\{E(S_2) - E(S_1)\}$ is $8 - 2 = 6$ which is considerably larger than the corresponding differences for the other strategy pairs, $6 - 4 = 2$ and $6 - 5 = 1$. In most realistic decision problems, the weak dominance criterion is likely to satisfy the transitivity requirement and its use will not present difficulties.

The above example can also be used to demonstrate that weak dominance in terms of payoffs is equivalent to weak dominance in terms of regret. The regret matrix corresponding to the payoff matrix given in Figure 8.2 is shown in Figure 8.3.

States of Nature

Strategy	N_1	N_2	N_3
S_1	0	10	28
S_2	8	0	24
S_3	5	15	0

Figure 8.3 Regret Matrix

Applying result (8.2) to differences between corresponding regrets yields: max $\{E(S_1) - E(S_2)\} = 2$ and max $\{E(S_2) - E(S_1)\} = 8$. Since $2 < 8$, S_1 dominates weakly S_2, as the decision maker prefers S_1 which has a smaller maximum expected difference in terms of regret relative to S_2, than S_2 relative to S_1. Moreover, from Figure 8.2 partial averages of differences between payoffs with respect to S_1 are: $\bar{D}_1 = 8$, $\bar{D}_2 = -1$ and $\bar{D}_3 = -2$, and therefore, max $\{E(S_1) - E(S_2)\} = 8$. Partial averages of the differences between payoffs with respect to S_2 are $\bar{D}_1 = -8$, $\bar{D}_2 = 1$ and $\bar{D}_3 = 2$, and therefore, max $\{E(S_2) - E(S_1)\} = 2$. As $8 > 2$, S_1 dominates weakly S_2. Notice also that max $\{E(S_2) - E(S_1)\} = 2$ is the same as $-$ min $\{E(S_1) - E(S_2)\} = -(-2) = 2$ which confirms result (8.4), and that in terms of payoffs min $\{E(S_1) - E(S_2)\} = -2$ is the same as $-$ max $\{E(S_1) - E(S_2)\} = -(2) = -2$ in terms of regret, which confirms result (8.9). As the numerical results which determine weak dominance are the same for payoffs and regret, the two criteria are equivalent.

8.6 CONCLUSIONS

It was shown above that the methodology developed in chapter 3 can be readily employed to define a criterion of weak statistical dominance which attempts to evaluate the attractiveness of one strategy in relation to another. Such a comparison is often of primary interest to decision makers. The fact that strict statistical dominance is a special case of weak statistical dominance increases the usefulness of the concept, for the two types of dominance can be evaluated simultaneously. The same applies to the equivalence of weak dominance in terms of payoffs and regret. Thus the results of chapter 3, 4 and 5, which are mainly concerned with evaluating strategies in isolation, are supplemented by the concept of weak statistical dominance which assesses a strategy in relation to other strategies.

9 Constrained games against nature

9.1 INTRODUCTION

The aim of this chapter[1] is to reformulate the decision maker's problem
discussed in chapter 3 as a constrained game against nature and to show
that the results obtained there are special cases of the more general
solutions presented here. The reformulation places the results obtained
earlier in a broader framework and highlights several aspects of the
problem which were not fully discussed previously. Compared with the
procedures developed in chapter 3, the new approach offers the decision
maker an important advantage. It enables him to adopt mixed strategies
using maximin and other criteria applied to expected payoffs. The
facility extends the scope and usefulness of the approach to decision
making developed in this book.

It is shown in section 9.2 that if the decision maker wishes to
consider mixed strategies and assumes that nature is hostile to him, his
decision problem may be represented as a two-person-zero-sum game against
nature. Characteristics of the general solution to such a problem are
also discussed, i.e. when it is assumed that the decision maker employs
the maximin criterion applied to expected payoffs and nature uses the
minimax criterion. In section 9.3 a constrained game against nature is
described which incorporates a weak ranking of probabilities of states
of nature. A general solution to the game is obtained and it is shown
that a special case of the solution corresponds to the results obtained
in section 3.4. In section 9.4 a constrained game against nature
incorporating strict ranking of probabilities is discussed and it is
demonstrated that a special case of the general solution of the game
agrees with the results obtained in section 3.5. A number of issues
relating to the interpretation of the results obtained earlier and their
usefulness are discussed in section 9.5. A possible application of the
theory to the investment portfolio selection problem is also investigated.
The case of benevolent nature is discussed in section 9.6. A numerical
illustration based on the investment portfolio selection problem is given
in section 9.7 in order to facilitate the use of the results in applied
work and to highlight a number of relationships which exist between the
special cases discussed in this chapter.

9.2 TWO-PERSON-ZERO-SUM GAME AGAINST NATURE

The framework of the decision problem considered here is similar to the
one described in chapter 3, i.e. the decision maker has S_i, i = 1,2....m,
mutually exclusive and exhaustive strategies to choose from; there are
N_j, j = 1, 2....n, mutually exclusive and exhaustive states of nature;
and X_{ij} is the payoff corresponding to a combination of S_i and N_j. In
chapter 3, the decision maker had to select one of the strategies open
to him and it was generally assumed that nature neither helped nor
hindered him consciously. Adopting the usual approach of the theory of
games, it is now assumed that nature acts as a conscious opponent of the
decision maker, and that any gains accruing to the decision maker are
equal to nature's losses and vice versa, i.e. the sum of the gains and

losses is zero. It is also assumed that now the decision maker can adopt mixed strategies, i.e. he can decide to select the strategy S_i with probability Q_i etc. Nature was allowed to use mixed strategies in chapter 3, because it was assumed that P_j was the probability of occurrence of states of nature N_j, etc. The characteristics of the decision problem described above represent quite adequately the viewpoint of a cautious decision maker. He wants to be prepared for the worst eventuality, i.e. he wishes to assume that nature is hostile to him. In spite of this, he is not prepared to rely on the complete ignorance criteria, but prefers to use the maximin criterion applied to expected payoffs. This is particularly so when he believes that he possesses some information about the probabilities with which the states of nature are likely to occur.

As an introduction to the game theory approach to decision making, it is assumed first that no restrictions are placed on the Q_i and the P_j, i.e. each of these can take any value between 0 and 1, subject only to the proviso that $\sum_{i=1}^{m} Q_i = \sum_{j=1}^{n} P_j = 1$. For any fixed set of Q_i and P_j, it is possible to define the value of the game to the decision maker as:

$$F = \sum_{i=1}^{m} \sum_{j=1}^{n} Q_i X_{ij} P_j \qquad (9.1)$$

where F is the expected payoff which he will secure in the long run if the game is repeated many times and strategies are selected with probabilities Q_i and states of nature occur with probabilities P_j.

The classic game theory problem arises when nature behaves as a conscious opponent of the decision maker and chooses the P_j in such a way as to make F as small as possible, while the decision maker selects his Q_i in such a way as to make F as large as possible. Both players have the same information at their disposal and are intelligent, so that they can always be relied upon to adopt the most effective mixed strategy in response to any given action of the opponent. Von Neumann and Morgenstern (1947) have shown that in these conditions there exists an optimal set of P_j and an optimal set of Q_i which yield an optimal value of the game F^*. The value is optimal and stable in the sense that neither the decision maker nor nature can move away from their respective optimal sets of probabilities without enabling the opponent to change his strategy in reply, thus securing a more favourable position for himself. To reach the stable solution of the game, the decision maker uses the maximin criterion for selecting his optimal mixed strategy, i.e. he finds a mixed strategy to which nature's best reply yields F^* as the value of the game. If he adopts any other mixed strategy, nature can select a counter strategy which will produce a value of the game less than F^*. Thus, the strategy which yields F^* as the value of the game, is the maximin strategy of the decision maker, i.e. it yields the maximum of the minimum values to which nature can confine him. It can also be viewed as giving the highest 'floor' in the F value which the decision maker can secure irrespective of any counter action nature can offer.

Nature's objectives are just the opposite. It uses the minimax criterion to find its optimal mixed strategy. It examines all the maximum expected payoffs which the decision maker can secure for himself, given the various mixed strategies it can adopt, and selects the one producing the smallest of these. In other words, it finds the lowest possible 'ceiling' for the expected payoff, C^*, say, beyond which the value of the game cannot be increased no matter which strategy the decision maker adopts.

The fundamental theorem of the two-person-zero-sum game states that if the decision maker employs the maximin criterion and nature uses the minimax criterion, they reach a stable solution where $F^* = C^*$. They will maintain this position because as soon as one of them adopts a different strategy, the opponent can retaliate by changing his strategy, making the position of his adversary worse than it was initially.

The problems facing the decision maker and nature can be represented by a pair of linear programmes whose solutions provide a proof of the fundamental result first obtained by von Neumann and Morgenstern using a different procedure. The problem facing the decision maker can be represented by the following linear programme:

Maximise $\quad F$

subject to $\quad \displaystyle\sum_{i=1}^{m} Q_i X_{ij} - F \geqslant 0 \qquad (j = 1, 2 \ldots n)$

$\qquad\qquad \displaystyle\sum_{i=1}^{m} Q_i = 1, \quad Q_i \geqslant 0 \qquad (i = 1, 2 \ldots m) \qquad (9.2)$

where Q_i and F are the variables. The decision maker is trying to select the Q_i in such a way as to reach the highest value of F, the 'floor', below which nature cannot push him down, irrespective of the strategy it employs. Notice that the n inequality constraints of (9.2) ensure that if nature were to adopt a pure strategy, the expected payoff of the game would be equal to or greater than F^*, the solution to the linear programme (9.2). Note also that the n inequality constraints of (9.2) are equivalent to

$$\sum_{j=1}^{n} P_j \sum_{i=1}^{m} Q_i X_{ij} \geqslant \sum_{j=1}^{n} P_j F$$

or

$$\sum_{j=1}^{n} \sum_{i=1}^{m} P_j Q_i X_{ij} \geqslant F \qquad \text{as} \quad \sum_{j=1}^{n} P_j = 1 \qquad (9.3)$$

Result (9.3) shows that the solution to linear programme (9.2) ensures that the expected payoff of the game is equal to or is larger than the optimum value, irrespective of the mixed strategy nature decides to use.

The situation facing nature may be represented by a similar linear programme:

Minimise $\quad C$

subject to $\quad \displaystyle\sum_{j=1}^{n} P_j X_{ij} - C \leqslant 0 \qquad (i = 1, 2 \ldots m)$

$\qquad\qquad \displaystyle\sum_{j=1}^{n} P_j = 1, \quad P_j \geqslant 0 \qquad (j = 1, 2 \ldots n) \qquad (9.4)$

where P_j and C are the variables. Nature's objective is to find a set of P_j yielding the minimum value of C, C^* (ceiling) which ensures that no matter which strategy the decision maker adopts, the expected payoff of the game will be less than or equal to C^*, i.e. nature employs the minimax principle.

It can be readily verified that linear programme (9.4) is the dual of (9.2), and it follows that optimal values of the two objective functions are equal, i.e. $F^* = C^*$. In general, the solutions to problems (9.2) and (9.4) exist and are non-trivial and, therefore, a stable value of the game always exists. This result proves the von Neumann-Morgenstern theorem of the two-person-zero-sum game.

An important implication of the above results is that a decision maker facing the same or a similar decision problem repeatedly and believing that nature is hostile to him, can determine an optimal mixed strategy, i.e. an optimal set Q_i, by solving the linear programme (9.2). He can then be confident that his average payoff in the long run will be larger than the average payoff he would have secured if he had selected a different strategy. In particular, he will do better in the long run than if he had selected a pure strategy using the same maximin criterion (as he was advised to do in chapter 3) because a pure strategy is a special case of the more general mixed strategy.

The solution of the linear programme (9.4) gives the optimal set of P_j for nature to use in order to restrict the decision maker's long run average payoff to the minimum, i.e. C^*. If nature fails to choose its optimal strategy, and the decision maker realises this, he can change his strategy and increase his expected payoff in the long run.

9.3   CONSTRAINED GAMES AGAINST NATURE - THE CASE OF WEAK RANKING OF
      PROBABILITIES

If information, additional to that incorporated in the linear programmes (9.2) and (9.4), is available about the probabilities of the payoffs, and it can be expressed as linear constraints, then the resulting pair of linear programmes constitutes a constrained game, a term due to Charnes and Cooper (1961). It was pointed out in chapter 3 and subsequently, that a reasonable assumption is that the decision maker can specify a weak ranking of probabilities of states of nature, i.e. $P_j - P_{j+1} \geq 0$ for $j = 1, 2....(n-1)$. When this is done, the mixed strategies which hostile nature can adopt will be restricted to the probability distributions satisfying the ranking constraint. Thus, in this case, nature will be a less formidable opponent than in the unconstrained case discussed in section 9.2, and the expected payoff of the game to the decision maker should, in general, be larger.

If it is assumed that nature still uses the minimax principle, its situation is now represented by the following linear programme:

Minimise C

subject to $\sum_{j=1}^{n} P_j X_{ij} - C \leq 0$ $(i = 1, 2....m)$

$\qquad\qquad P_j - P_{j+1} \geq 0$ $(j = 1, 2....(n-1))$

$\qquad\qquad \sum_{j=1}^{n} P_j = 1 \quad P_j \geq 0$ $(j = 1, 2....n)$ (9.5) where P_j and C are the variables.

The dual of linear programme (9.5) represents the problem facing the decision maker and is given by:

<u>Maximise</u>   F

$$\underline{\text{subject to}} \sum_{i=1}^{m} Q_i X_{i1} - R_1 \qquad - F \geqslant 0$$

$$\sum_{i=1}^{m} Q_i X_{i2} + R_1 - R_2 - F \geqslant 0$$

$$\begin{matrix} \cdot & \cdot & \cdot & \cdot & \cdot \\ \cdot & \cdot & \cdot & \cdot & \cdot \\ \cdot & \cdot & \cdot & \cdot & \cdot \end{matrix}$$

$$\sum_{i=1}^{m} Q_i X_{ij} + R_{j-1} - R_j - F \geqslant 0$$

$$\begin{matrix} \cdot & \cdot & \cdot & \cdot & \cdot \\ \cdot & \cdot & \cdot & \cdot & \cdot \\ \cdot & \cdot & \cdot & \cdot & \cdot \end{matrix}$$

$$\sum_{i=1}^{m} Q_i X_{in} + R_{n-1} \qquad - F \geqslant 0$$

$$\sum_{i=1}^{m} Q_i \quad = \quad 1$$

$$Q_i \geqslant 0 (i=1,2....m); \quad R_j \quad \geqslant \quad 0 \; (j = 1....(n-1)) \qquad (9.6)$$

where Q_i, R_j and F are the variables. The R_j correspond to the constraints representing weak ranking of probabilities in (9.5). When the decision maker wants to find his optimal strategy and the optimal expected payoff, it is only necessary to solve linear programme (9.6). When interest centres on nature's optimal strategy, the solution to linear programme (9.5) is required.

It is also possible to examine some properties of the general solutions of linear programmes (9.5) and (9.6) using the theorem of complementary slackness linking the primal and dual. The theorem states that if $P_j > 0$ at the optimum, the corresponding slack variable in the dual is equal to zero, and therefore, the constraint in the dual corresponding to it becomes an equation. Assume now that at the optimum $P_j > 0$ for $j = 1$, $2....k$, and $P_j = 0$ for $j = k+1$, ...n. Note also that because of ranking, if $P_k > 0$, $P_j > 0$, $j = 1$, $2....(k-1)$, and if $P_{k+1} = 0$, $P_j = 0$, $j = k+2$, ...n. If the above conditions are satisfied, the inequality constraints on the probability differences, $P_j - P_{j+1}$, for $j = k$, $(k+1)$ ....(n-1), are redundant at the optimum, and therefore, $R_j = 0$ for $j = k$, $k+1$ .... (n-1). Notice also, that the constraint $P_k - P_{k+1} \geqslant 0$ reduces to $P_k \geqslant 0$ as $P_{k+1} = 0$ and is the same as the non-negativity constraint which all P_j must satisfy. Thus, the constraints in the dual (9.6) corresponding to positive P_j become equations, giving:

$$\sum_{i=1}^{m} Q_i X_{i1} \quad - R_1 \qquad = F$$

$$\sum_{i=1}^{m} Q_i X_{i2} \quad + R_1 \quad - R_2 \quad = F$$

$$\cdots \cdots \quad \cdot \quad \cdot$$
$$\cdots \cdots \quad \cdot \quad \cdot$$
$$\cdots \cdots \quad \cdot \quad \cdot$$

$$\sum_{i=1}^{m} Q_i X_{i,k-1} \quad + R_{k-2} \quad - R_{k-1} \quad = F$$

$$\sum_{i=1}^{m} Q_i X_{ik} \quad + R_{k-1} \qquad = F \qquad (9.7)$$

Summing equations (9.7) at the optimum, we get:

$$kF^* = \sum_{i=1}^{m} \sum_{j=1}^{k} Q_i X_{ij} \quad \text{or} \quad F^* = \frac{1}{k} \sum_{i=1}^{m} \sum_{j=1}^{k} Q_i X_{ij} \qquad (9.8)$$

Since the value of the objective function of the primal and the dual is the same at the optimum, we also have $F^* = C^*$. Result (9.8) is not a complete solution to the linear programme (9.6) because it incorporates the Q_i which still have to be determined. This can only be done by solving linear programme (9.6). It is also worth noting that, as in the case of the unconstrained game discussed in section 9.2, $F^* = C^*$, i.e. the 'floor' and the 'ceiling' coincide at the optimum. The interpretation of the dual variables R_j is considered in section 9.5 because they also appear in the constrained games with strict probability ranking to be discussed in section 9.4, and play the same role in both situations.

Special case If the decision maker considers only pure strategies and applies the maximin principle, as he did in chapter 3, this is equivalent to setting $Q_i = 1$ in result (9.8) and the other Q's equal to zero. Given these assumptions, (9.8) reduces to:

$$F^* = \frac{1}{k} \sum_{j=1}^{k} X_{ij} \qquad (9.9)$$

which is equivalent to result (3.11) in chapter 3. In result (9.9), i refers to the pure strategy which yields the highest minimum expected payoff and k identifies the partial average of payoffs which yields the minimum expected payoff of the strategy.

9.4 CONSTRAINED GAMES AGAINST NATURE - THE CASE OF STRICT RANKING OF PROBABILITIES

The situation considered here is similar to that discussed in section 9.3, but it is now assumed that the decision maker can specify a strict ranking of probabilities of the forthcoming states of nature, i.e. he can specify the constants K_j in the expressions $P_j - P_{j+1} \geqslant K_j$ for $j = 1, 2 \ldots n$ where $P_{n+1} = 0$ by definition. As $\sum_{j=1}^{n} P_j = 1$, the K_j

must be so chosen as to satisfy the condition $\sum_{j=1}^{n} j\, K_j \leqslant 1$. Identical
assumptions were made in section 3.5.

Assuming that nature still uses the minimax criterion to select its
optimum strategy, its situation can be represented by the following
linear programme:

<u>Minimise</u>   C

<u>subject to</u> $\sum_{j=1}^{n} P_j X_{ij} - C \leqslant 0$ $(i = 1, 2....m)$

$P_j - P_{j+1} \geqslant K_j$ $(j = 1, 2....n)$

$\sum_{j=1}^{n} P_j = 1, \quad P_j \geqslant 0 \quad (j = 1, 2....n)$ (9.10)

As compared with linear programme (9.5), problem (9.10) incorporates
strict ranking of the P_j and the number of ranking constraints is now n
because $P_n - P_{n+1} \geqslant K_n$, or $P_n \geqslant K_n$ (as $P_{n+1} = 0$) is a substantive
constraint.

The dual of (9.10) represents the problem facing the decision maker and
is given by:

<u>Maximise</u> $F + \sum_{j=1}^{n} K_j R_j$

<u>subject to</u> $\sum_{i=1}^{m} Q_i X_{i1} - R_1 \qquad\qquad - F \geqslant 0$

$\sum_{i=1}^{m} Q_i X_{i2} + R_1 \qquad - R_2 - F \geqslant 0$

. . .   . .
. . .   . .
. . .   . .

$\sum_{i=1}^{m} Q_i X_{ij} + R_{j-1} - R_j - F \geqslant 0$

. . .   . .
. . .   . .
. . .   . .

$\sum_{i=1}^{m} Q_i X_{in} + R_{n-1} - R_n - F \geqslant 0$

$\sum_{i=1}^{m} Q_i = 1$

$Q_i \geqslant 0 \ (i = 1....m \ ); \quad R_j \geqslant 0 \quad (i = 1, 2....n)$ (9.11)

R_j are the dual variables corresponding to the n strict ranking
constraints imposed on the P_j in (9.10). Notice that, as compared with
(9.6), there is an additional dual variable, R_n, in (9.11). This is due
to the fact that the constraint $P_n - P_{n+1} \geqslant K_n$ in (9.10) is a substantive

constraint and not simply a non-negativity constraint as it was in (9.5). In order to find the maximin mixed strategy for the decision maker, it is only necessary to solve (9.11). If the interest centres on the minimax strategy of nature, it can be found by solving (9.10).

As in the preceding section, it is possible to examine some properties of the general solution of (9.10) and (9.11) using the theorem on complementary slackness linking the primal and the dual. Suppose that in problem (9.10) the last strictly positive K is K_g, then at least the first g P_j must be strictly positive because of the ranking and, therefore, by the theorem of complementary slackness, the first g dual constraints corresponding to them in (9.11) hold as equations at the optimum, i.e.

$$\sum_{i=1}^{m} Q_i X_{i1} - R_1 \qquad - F = 0$$

$$\sum_{i=1}^{m} Q_i X_{i2} + R_1 \quad - R_2 - F = 0$$

$$\begin{matrix} \cdot & \cdot & \cdot & \cdot & \cdot \\ \cdot & \cdot & \cdot & \cdot & \cdot \\ \cdot & \cdot & \cdot & \cdot & \cdot \end{matrix}$$

$$\sum_{i=1}^{m} Q_i X_{ig} + R_{g-1} - R_g - F = 0 \qquad\qquad (9.12)$$

Using equations (9.12) to express the R_j in terms of the other variables, we have:

$$R_1 = \sum_{i=1}^{m} Q_i X_{i1} - F = \sum_{i=1}^{m} Q_i Y_{i1} - F, \text{ where } Y_{ij} = \sum_{k=1}^{j} X_{ik}$$

$$R_2 = \sum_{i=1}^{m} Q_i X_{i1} + \sum_{i=1}^{m} Q_i X_{i2} - 2F = \sum_{i=1}^{m} Q_i Y_{i2} - 2F$$

$$\begin{matrix} \cdot & \cdot & \cdot & \cdot & \cdot & \cdot \\ \cdot & \cdot & \cdot & \cdot & \cdot & \cdot \\ \cdot & \cdot & \cdot & \cdot & \cdot & \cdot \end{matrix}$$

$$R_g = \sum_{i=1}^{m} Q_i X_{i1} + \sum_{i=1}^{m} Q_i X_{i2} + \ldots + \sum_{i=1}^{m} Q_i X_{ig} - gF = \sum_{i=1}^{m} Q_i Y_{ig} - gF$$

$$(9.13)$$

Note also that since it was assumed above that $K_j = 0$ for $j = g+1, \ldots n$, the objective function in (9.11) is given at the optimum by:

$$Z = F + \sum_{j=1}^{g} K_j R_j \qquad\qquad (9.14)$$

where Z is the value of the objective function. Substituting for R_j from (9.13) into (9.14) we have

$$Z = F + K_1 (\sum_{i=1}^{m} Q_i Y_{i1} - F) + K_2 (\sum_{i=1}^{m} Q_i Y_{i2} - 2F) + \ldots$$

$$+ K_g (\sum_{i=1}^{m} Q_i Y_{ig} - gF)$$

$$= F (1 - \sum_{j=1}^{g} jK_j) + \sum_{j=1}^{g} K_j \sum_{i=1}^{m} Q_i Y_{ij} \qquad (9.15)$$

We note now that, in the case of weak ranking of probabilities, $K_j = 0$ for $j = 1, 2 \ldots n$ and therefore, (9.15) reduces to $Z = F$. Moreover, it was shown in section 9.3 that in this case the optimum value of the objective function is given by (9.8) which can be also written as:

$$F = \frac{1}{k} \sum_{i=1}^{m} \sum_{j=1}^{k} Q_i X_{ij} = \frac{1}{k} \sum_{i=1}^{m} Q_i Y_{ik} \qquad (9.16)$$

where $Y_{ik} = \sum_{j=1}^{k} X_{ij}$. Substituting (9.16) into (9.15) we obtain a general result for the optimum value of Z:

$$Z^* = (\frac{1}{k} \sum_{i=1}^{m} Q_i Y_{ik})(1 - \sum_{j=1}^{n} jK_j) + \sum_{j=1}^{n} K_j \sum_{i=1}^{m} Q_i Y_{ij} \qquad (9.17)$$

Notice that the range of summation in result (9.15) over the j subscript has been extended from g to n before the substitution for F was made. The change is legitimate in the specific case discussed above, because $K_j = 0$ for $j = g+1, \ldots n$, and it also covers the possibility that $g = n$ to begin with. Note also that result (9.17) depends on the optimum Q_i which can only be found by solving the specific linear programme (9.11). Since the optimum value of the objective function of the primal and the dual is the same, $Z^* = C^*$.

Special Case 1 When weak ranking of probabilities is assumed, i.e. when $K_j = 0$ for $j = 1, 2 \ldots n$, (9.17) reduces to (9.8), as one would expect.

Special Case 2 When only pure strategies are available to the decision maker, i.e. when $Q_i = 1$ and the other Q's are zero, (9.17) reduces to:

$$Z^* = (\frac{1}{k} Y_{ik})(1 - \sum_{j=1}^{n} jK_j) + \sum_{j=1}^{n} K_j Y_{ij}$$

which is the same as result (3.16) in chapter 3, because the partial average $\frac{1}{k} Y_{ik}$ can also be written as $\frac{1}{j} Y_{ij}$, and because the suffix i was suppressed in (3.16).

9.5   INTERPRETATION AND POSSIBLE APPLICATIONS OF THE RESULTS

This section deals with the interpretation of the dual variables R_j appearing in linear programmes (9.6) and (9.11) in sections 9.3 and 9.4 respectively, the implications of weak and strict ranking for nature's game, the use of mixed strategies in practical decision making and the application of constrained games against nature to the investment portfolio selection problem.

Bearing in mind the relationship between the optimum values of the dual variables and the primal constraints to which they correspond, it is possible to interpret the additional dual variables R_j appearing in expressions (9.6) and (9.11) in the following way. The optimum value of R_j measures the marginal gain or loss in the optimal expected value of the game associated respectively with the increase or decrease in the minimum probability difference K_j at the optimum. Since the R_j are positive by definition, if, for example, K_j is increased by a small amount ΔK_j, the optimum value of the objective function will be increased by $R_j \Delta K_j$. Thus, if the decision maker is able to specify the minimum difference between the probabilities $P_j - P_{j+1}$ more precisely, e.g. by increasing K_j to $K_j + \Delta K_j$, the value of the game is increased by $R_j \Delta K_j$ at the optimum. This interpretation is valid as long as the probability distribution applicable at the optimum remains unaltered by the small change in K_j. If it does not, it is necessary to solve the modified linear programme afresh. The same happens in the case of weak ranking of probabilities. An optimum value of R_j shows how much the expected value will increase at the optimum when the minimum difference $P_j - P_{j+1}$ increases from zero to ΔK_j. Again the increase will be $R_j \Delta K_j$. In both cases the increase in K_j eliminates some probability distributions, which nature could previously use, and thus enables the decision maker to increase the value of the game or, in the worst case, to leave it unchanged. If a constraint $P_j - P_{j+1} \geqslant K_j$ is not binding at the optimum, then the slack variable associated with the constraint is positive and, due to the theorem of complementary slackness, $R_j = 0$, indicating that there is no potential gain to the decision maker at the margin from increasing K_j.

It was mentioned in section 9.2 that the optimum expected payoff will, in general, be larger in the case of the constrained game involving weak ranking of probabilities than in the case of the unconstrained game. It was also pointed out in section 9.4 that the value of the game, when strict ranking of probabilities is involved, is, in general, larger than when weak ranking of probabilities arises. This happens because, as compared with the unconstrained game, nature's capacity to retaliate to any move made by the decision maker is progressively restricted as weak and strict ranking are introduced. At each step the range of mixed strategies (probability distributions) open to nature is reduced, and thus the decision maker is able to increase the value of the game (the 'floor') below which nature cannot beat him down. In the case of the unconstrained game discussed in section 9.2, the value of the game is so determined that if nature chooses one of its pure strategies, the expected payoff will be larger than or equal to the value of the game. When weak ranking of probabilities is introduced, nature can no longer select any pure strategy it wishes. It can still choose the most likely state of nature with probability $P_1 = 1$, but the other states of nature cannot be chosen as pure strategies because of the weak ranking constraint. For example, if the second state of nature is particularly unattractive to the decision maker, nature cannot choose it as a pure strategy because the maximum value of P_2 is restricted to $\frac{1}{2}$ by the weak ranking constraint, which requires that P_1 is at least equal to P_2. These constraints limit the retaliatory capacity of nature to any moves made by the decision maker, and thus enable him to find a better mixed strategy and secure a higher value of the game than in the unconstrained case. When strict ranking of probabilities is introduced, nature's freedom of manoeuvre is restricted even more and the decision maker can

increase the value of the game still further. Now, nature can choose
only mixed strategies, unless $K_j = 0$, $j = 2, 3 \ldots n$ when the most likely
state of nature can be chosen as a pure strategy. It can be readily
shown that in the case of strict probability ranking

$$\max P_j = \frac{1}{j}(1 - \sum_{r=1}^{j-1} rK_r - \sum_{r=j+1}^{n} rK_r) \quad (j = 1, 2 \ldots n) \qquad (9.18)$$

The use of a number of relationships discussed above and result (9.18)
will be illustrated in section 9.7.

The constrained game approach to decision making has an important
advantage as compared with the methodology developed in chapter 3.
Previously, the decision maker was limited to the choice of pure
strategies. Now, he can adopt mixed strategies, if they happen to be
more advantageous to him than pure strategies. In general, mixed
strategies provide him with a better protection against hostile nature
than do pure strategies. As the optimum expected payoff for the
constrained game is greater than or equal to the maximin expected payoff
obtained when using pure strategies (c.f. chapter 3) the decision maker
employing mixed strategies will be better off in the long run, if he
faces the same decision problem many times. In practice it is unlikely
that the same decision problem will arise on many occasions. But even if
the decision maker faces a series of decision problems where the number
of states of nature, their probability ranking and payoff matrix change
from problem to problem, the use of the optimum mixed strategies derived
from the solution of constrained games of the type described in sections
9.3 and 9.4 will yield a higher average payoff in the long run than the
selection of a pure strategy yielding the maximin expected payoff. This
general conclusion is based on the assumption that nature is always
malevolently disposed towards the decision maker, and that he is prepared
to accept the risk that occasionally his decision will result in a very
low payoff. In the long run the unfavourable outcome of a decision will
be more than offset by favourable results.

The constrained game approach to decision making discussed in sections
9.3 and 9.4 appears to have a ready application to the investment
portfolio selection problem. In this case, the investor usually has some
beliefs about the probabilities of the forthcoming states of nature which
may take the form of weak or strict ranking of probabilities, and he often
wants to be prepared for the worst circumstances that may arise in the
future. If his pure strategies correspond to purchases of different
types of securities or different shares, his objective is to select an
optimal mix of these so that his portfolio of shares performs well in the
most unfavourable conditions that nature may have in store for him. In
the more formal language of sections 9.3 and 9.4, he wishes to employ the
maximin principle to select the mix of securities with the highest
possible expected return, the 'floor', below which nature cannot force
him no matter which of the allowable probability distributions it uses.
In normal circumstances, when the optimal mixed strategy is determined,
the decision maker selects a pure strategy using the optimum set of
probabilities in the selection process, i.e. strategy S_i has the
probability Q_i^* of being selected, etc. In the case of the portfolio
selection problem, the investor does not have to locate all his funds in
a single share appropriately selected, but he can actually invest in all
shares being considered, distributing his funds between them according to
the optimal probabilities, i.e. proportion Q_i^* of the total fund will be

invested in share i, etc. This facility ensures that if the same or
similar investment decisions are taken many times, the average expected
return on investment obtained by the decision maker at successive stages
will approach the theoretical optimum return more rapidly than when all
the funds are invested in one share selected according to the optimum
probabilities. In this type of problem, the variation in the return on
investment between strategies (shares) is eliminated, because the
investor can actually purchase the optimum mix of shares. The
discrepancy between the actual average return on investment secured at
any one time and the optimum expected return predicted by the theory will
be due only to variation between different states of nature. The above
analysis is based on the assumption that nature is consistently
malevolent. Thus it should suit a cautious investor interested primarily
in a defensive portfolio. If he does not believe that nature is
consistently malevolent, he should look at the case of benevolent nature
discussed in the following section and devise a compromise mixed strategy.
A numerical illustration based on the investment portfolio selection
problem is described in section 9.7.

9.6   THE CASE OF BENEVOLENT NATURE

So far in this chapter it was assumed that nature acts as a conscious
opponent of the decision maker, i.e. it strives to limit his expected
payoff to the minimum. Such a view may suit a pessimistic or cautious
decision maker, but may be unattractive to an optimistic or adventurous
one. Moreover, in classical decision theory nature plays a neutral role,
i.e. it neither consciously favours the decision maker nor hinders him.
It is interesting to consider, therefore, whether the constrained game
theory approach to decision making can be adapted to incorporate the
case of benevolent nature.

The natural thing to do is to reformulate linear programmes (9.4),
(9.5) and (9.10) which represent the position of malevolent nature. If
the decision maker believes that nature is favourably disposed towards
him, he can assume that it uses the maximin rather than the minimax
criterion to select its optimal mixed strategy. In this case the
situation facing nature may be represented by the following linear
programme corresponding to problem (9.10) and incorporating strict
ranking of probabilities:

$$\text{\underline{Maximise}} \quad C$$

$$\text{\underline{subject to}} \quad \sum_{j=1}^{n} P_j X_{ij} - C \geq 0 \qquad\qquad (i = 1, 2 \ldots m)$$

$$P_j - P_{j+1} \geq K_j \qquad\qquad (j = 1, 2 \ldots n)$$

$$\sum_{j=1}^{n} P_j = 1, \quad P_j \geq 0 \qquad (j = 1, 2 \ldots n) \quad (9.19)$$

It is possible to write the dual of the above problem which will represent
the situation facing the decision maker and to obtain a general solution
analogous to the one obtained in result (9.17). This will not be done
here because formulation (9.19) and its dual are based on an implicit
assumption which negates the benevolent character of nature.

The difficulty arises because the solutions to the problem (9.19) and its dual are based on the assumption that nature and the decision maker oppose each other. Nature now tries to ensure that the expected payoff is as high as possible while the decision maker tries to keep it as low as possible. In this case C*, the optimum value of the objective function in (9.19) becomes a 'floor' below which the value of the game cannot be reduced by the uncooperative decision maker, however perverse his choice of mixed strategies. Since some of the strategies open to the decision maker may be very unfavourable to him, the optimum expected payoff, C*, which nature can secure for him can be lower than the value of the game he can secure for himself, when he tries to do his best against malevolent nature. Such a solution is obviously of little value because in the case of benevolent nature, the decision maker is supposed to cooperate with it and is expected to secure a higher expected payoff than in the case of malevolent nature.

A more appropriate formulation of the problem to represent the case of benevolent nature is as follows:

$$\underline{\text{Maximise}} \quad \sum_{i=1}^{m} \sum_{j=1}^{n} Q_i X_{ij} P_j = \sum_{i=1}^{m} Q_i \sum_{j=1}^{n} P_j X_{ij}$$

$$\underline{\text{subject to}} \quad P_j - P_{j+1} \geq K_j, \qquad (j = 1, 2 \ldots n)$$

$$\sum_{j=1}^{n} P_j = 1, \qquad P_j \geq 0 \ (j = 1, 2 \ldots n)$$

$$\sum_{i=1}^{m} Q_i = 1, \qquad Q_i \geq 0 \ (i = 1, 2 \ldots m) \qquad (9.20)$$

Here Q_i and P_j are the variables which have to be determined in such a way as to maximise the expected payoff. Such a formulation assumes that the decision maker and nature cooperate in order to maximise the value of the game.

Expressions (9.20) represent a quadratic programming problem, which is often difficult to solve. Fortunately in this case the solution can be readily identified. The second formulation of the objective function in (9.20) shows that it is a weighted average of expected payoffs of individual strategies, where Q_i are used as weights. It is clear, therefore, that the expected payoff will be maximised when a maximum weight, i.e. 1, is allocated to the strategy having the largest maximum expected payoff. Thus to secure the largest expected payoff, the decision maker has to select the strategy which potentially has the largest maximum expected payoff and then nature must benevolently ensure that the probability distribution producing the maximum expected payoff of the selected strategy is the operative one. Thus the solution to the problem is the maximax expected payoff of chapter 3 where only pure strategies were considered. Notice also that if no constraints are imposed on the probabilities of states of nature, the maximum value of the objective function of problem (9.20) will be equal to the maximum payoff in the payoff matrix. In this case the decision maker will choose the strategy with the maximum payoff and benevolent nature will obligingly ensure that the state of nature containing the maximum payoff occurs. This solution to the problem is the same as that obtained in chapter 2 under conditions of complete ignorance when the maximax payoff criterion was used to select a strategy.

Some decision makers will take the view that nature is neither consistently malevolent nor benevolent to them and may be inclined to assume that the true state of affairs lies somewhere between the two extremes. A natural thing for them to do would be to average the two probability distributions associated with the two extreme cases. The weight assigned to each can correspond to the degree of pessimism-optimism of the decision maker. For example, if the maximin mixed strategy is $Q_1 = \frac{1}{4}$, $Q_2 = \frac{1}{2}$ and $Q_3 = \frac{1}{4}$ and the maximax pure strategy is $Q_1 = 0$, $Q_2 = 0$, $Q_3 = 1$, and the decision maker, being more pessimistic than optimistic, decides to give a weight of $\frac{3}{4}$ to the first strategy and $\frac{1}{4}$ to the second, the compromise strategy will be $Q_1 = {}^3/_{16}$, $Q_2 = {}^6/_{16}$ and $Q_3 = {}^7/_{16}$.

9.7 A NUMERICAL ILLUSTRATION

In order to illustrate the methods developed in this chapter and to facilitate their assimilation, a numerical example will now be presented. A hypothetical investment portfolio selection problem will be used for the purpose.

Suppose an investor has a fixed sum of money at his disposal and is considering its location in three different shares. He can invest all the money in a single share, i.e. employ a pure strategy, or he can buy all three shares in varying proportions, i.e. use a mixed strategy. His pure strategies are S_1 = purchase of the first share, S_2 = purchase of the second share and S_3 = purchase of the third share. He considers the investment as short term and thinks that only three states of nature are relevant: N_1 = no change in economic activity, N_2 = slow improvement and N_3 = slow deterioration. He also estimates that the real percentage returns on the three shares in the different circumstances are as shown in Figure 9.1.

Strategy	State of Nature		
	N_1	N_2	N_3
S_1	2	6	1
S_2	1	2	3
S_3	4	3	2

Figure 9.1 Payoff Matrix of Returns on Investment

The investor is prepared to use expected return on investment as a measure of the attractiveness of a particular portfolio because he makes similar decisions regularly and is able to offset an occasional poor decision by the more successful ones. He is also a cautious person interested primarily in a sound defensive portfolio. It is natural for him to assume that nature will be hostile and to adopt the maximin criterion in selecting his portfolio of shares. He can also make different assumptions about the amount of information he has about the probabilities of the forthcoming states of nature. Three cases will be distinguished: (i) unconstrained probabilities, (ii) weak ranking of probabilities and (iii) strict ranking of probabilities. These were discussed fully in sections 9.2, 9.3 and 9.4 respectively.

(i) Unconstrained Probabilities

In this case no limitations are placed on the probabilities of the states of nature and the decision maker uses the maximin criterion to find his optimum mixed strategy. The situation facing him may be summarised by the following linear programme which corresponds to (9.2):

Maximise   F

subject to
$$2Q_1 + Q_2 + 4Q_3 - F \geq 0$$
$$6Q_1 + 2Q_2 + 3Q_3 - F \geq 0$$
$$Q_1 + 3Q_2 + 2Q_3 - F \geq 0$$
$$Q_1 + Q_2 + Q_3 = 1, \quad Q_i \geq 0, \qquad (i = 1, 2, 3) \qquad (9.21)$$

where Q_i and F are the variables whose optimal level has to be determined. Using the simplex technique or another method, it can be readily verified that the solution to (9.21) is $Q_1^* = 0$, $Q_2^* = \frac{1}{2}$, $Q_3^* = \frac{1}{2}$ and $F^* = 5/2$. Thus if the investor locates half of his investment funds in share 2 and half in share 3 his expected real return on investment will be at least $2\frac{1}{2}\%$, no matter which strategy nature adopts.

Notice that rather surprisingly the decision maker is advised not to invest in share 1 which could bring him the highest return possible, i.e. 6%. The advice is correct because return on share 1 is low when N_1 or N_3 occurs. If, for example, half of the money was invested in share 1 and half in share 2, the return on investment would be $1\frac{1}{2}\%$ if N_1 was certain to occur, and $1\frac{1}{2}\%$ is lower than the optimum return of $2\frac{1}{2}\%$. If half of the money was invested in share 1 and half in share 3, the return would again be $1\frac{1}{2}\%$ if N_3 was certain to occur; and once more the optimal strategy is superior, for it secures a return of $2\frac{1}{2}\%$ under the same conditions.

The situation facing nature may be represented by the following linear programme which is the dual of (9.21) and corresponds to (9.4):

Minimise   C

subject to
$$2P_1 + 6P_2 + P_3 - C \leq 0$$
$$P_1 + 2P_2 + 3P_3 - C \leq 0$$
$$4P_1 + 3P_2 + 2P_3 - C \leq 0$$
$$P_1 + P_2 + P_3 = 1, \quad P_j \geq 0, \qquad (j = 1, 2, 3) \qquad (9.22)$$

where P_j and C are the variables whose optimal level has to be determined. If the simplex method is used to solve (9.21), the optimal P_j in (9.22) are given by the coefficients (taken with the positive sign) of the slack variables in the final objective function. The optimal value of the objective function in (9.22) is the same as in (9.21), i.e. $C^* = 5/2$. In this case there are two sets of P_j which yield the optimal value of the objective function: $P_1^* = \frac{1}{4}$, $P_2^* = 0$, $P_3^* = \frac{3}{4}$ and $P_1^* = 2/18$, $P_2^* = 5/18$, $P_3^* = {}^{11}/18$. Notice that state of nature N_2 is rather favourable to the decision maker and, therefore, nature tries to keep its probability small,

i.e. $P_2^* = 0$ or $P_2^* = {}^5/_{18}$. If nature employs either one or the other
of its optimal strategies the best that the investor can do is to employ
his optimal strategy. If he does not, nature can revise its optimal
strategy and can ensure that the expected return on investment is reduced
below $2\frac{1}{2}\%$. If nature does not use its best strategy, the decision maker
can change his strategy and thus secure a return higher than $2\frac{1}{2}\%$.

(ii) Weak Ranking of Probabilities

If the investor believes that nature's probabilities are restricted by a
weak ranking constraint, i.e. $P_1 \geqslant P_2 \geqslant P_3$, he can take this into account
when selecting his portfolio. In this case it is more convenient to
start with the problem facing nature which corresponds to problem (9.5)
and is given by the following linear programme:

Minimise   C

subject to $2P_1 + 6P_2 + P_3 - C \leqslant 0$

$\quad\quad\quad\quad P_1 + 2P_2 + 3P_3 - C \leqslant 0$

$\quad\quad\quad 4P_1 + 3P_2 + 2P_3 - C \leqslant 0$

$\quad\quad\quad\quad P_1 - P_2 \quad\quad\quad\quad \geqslant 0$

$\quad\quad\quad\quad\quad\quad P_2 - P_3 \quad\quad \geqslant 0$

$\quad\quad\quad\quad P_1 + P_2 + P_3 \quad = 1, \; P_j \geqslant 0 \quad (j = 1, 2, 3) \quad\quad\quad (9.23)$

where P_j and C are the variables. Solving (9.23), we have $P_1^* = P_2^* =$
$P_3^* = {}^1/_3$ and $C^* = 3$.

The problem facing the decision maker is given by the following linear
programme which is the dual of (9.23) and is based on result (9.6):

Maximise   F

subject to $2Q_1 + Q_2 + 4Q_3 - R_1 \quad\quad - F \geqslant 0$

$\quad\quad\quad 6Q_1 + 2Q_2 + 3Q_3 + R_1 - R_2 - F \geqslant 0$

$\quad\quad\quad\quad Q_1 + 3Q_2 + 2Q_3 \quad\quad + R_2 - F \geqslant 0$

$\quad\quad\quad\quad Q_1 + Q_2 + Q_3 \quad\quad\quad\quad = 1$

$\quad\quad\quad\quad Q_i \geqslant 0 \; (i = 1, 2, 3) \; ; \; R_j \geqslant 0 \quad (j = 1, 2) \quad\quad\quad (9.24)$

where Q_1, Q_2, Q_3, R_1, R_2 and F are the variables. R_1 and R_2 are the
additional dual variables corresponding to the ranking constraints in
(9.23). The solution to the problem is $Q_1^* = \frac{1}{2}$, $Q_2^* = 0$, $Q_3^* = \frac{1}{2}$,
$R_1^* = 0$, $R_2^* = 1\frac{1}{2}$ and $F^* = 3$.

We note first, as compared with case (i), that the optimal mixed strategy
of the decision maker has changed. Previously, he invested half of his
funds in share 2 and half in share 3; now he invests half in share 1 and
half in share 3. This is what one would expect since N_1 and N_2 are now
more likely to occur and, therefore, share 1 offering payoffs 2 and 6
is now more attractive than share 2 with payoffs 1 and 2. Moreover, N_3
is now least likely and this again favours share 1 and makes share 2
less attractive. Share 3 with 4 and 3 as the more likely payoffs is

94

still a good proposition. Nature's best counter strategy is to make all its probabilities equal to $1/3$. As before, it tries to make P_3 large because N_3 is most unfavourable to the investor, but now it is unable to make P_3 larger than $1/3$ because of the ranking constraint. Nature is now unable to counter the moves of the investor as successfully as it did in the unconstrained case, and consequently the expected return on investment increases from $2\frac{1}{2}\%$ to 3%. As $R_1{}^* = 0$, the constraint $P_1 - P_2 \geqslant 0$ is not binding at the optimum. The fact that $R_2{}^* = 1\frac{1}{2}$ shows that if the minimum difference between P_2 and P_3 could be increased by a small amount ΔD, say, i.e. if the weak ranking constraint $P_2 - P_3 \geqslant 0$ could be replaced by a strict ranking constraint, $P_2 - P_3 \geqslant \Delta D$, the optimal expected return would increase by $1\frac{1}{2} \Delta D$.

(iii) Strict Ranking of Probabilities

If the investor is aware that nature's probabilities are subject to a strict ranking constraint, e.g. $P_1 - P_2 \geqslant \frac{1}{4}$ and $P_2 - P_3 \geqslant 1/8$, he can take this into account when selecting his portfolio and can improve his position still further. Again it is more convenient to start with the problem facing nature, which corresponds to problem (9.10) and is given by the following linear programme:

Minimise   C

subject to
$$
\begin{aligned}
2P_1 + 6P_2 + P_3 - C &\leqslant 0 \\
P_1 + 2P_2 + 3P_3 - C &\leqslant 0 \\
4P_1 + 3P_2 + 2P_3 - C &\leqslant 0 \\
P_1 - P_2 &\geqslant \tfrac{1}{4} \\
P_2 - P_3 &\geqslant 1/8 \\
P_1 + P_2 + P_3 &= 1, \quad P_j \geqslant 0, \ (j = 1,\,2,\,3) \qquad (9.25)
\end{aligned}
$$

where again P_j and C are the variables. The solution to (9.25) is $P_1{}^* = 13/24$, $P_2{}^* = 7/24$, $P_3{}^* = 4/24$ and $C^* = 3^3/8$. By employing this optimal strategy, nature can ensure that the investor's expected return on investment is confined to $3^3/8\%$. Knowing that N_3 is least favourable to the investor, nature once again tries to maximise P_3. Formula (9.18) may be used to verify that max $P_3 = 4/24 = 1/6$ when strict ranking of probabilities holds:

$$
\text{max } P_3 = 1/3 \ (1 - 1(\tfrac{1}{4}) - 2(1/8) - 0) = 1/6.
$$

The position of the investor is represented by the dual of (9.25) which corresponds to result (9.11) and is given by the following linear programme:

<u>Maximise</u> $F + \frac{1}{4}R_1 + 1/_8R_2$

<u>subject to</u> $2Q_1 + Q_2 + 4Q_3 - R_1 \quad - F \geqslant 0$
$\qquad\qquad 6Q_1 + 2Q_2 + 3Q_3 + R_1 - R_2 - F \geqslant 0$
$\qquad\qquad Q_1 + 3Q_2 + 2Q_3 \quad + R_2 - F \geqslant 0$
$\qquad\qquad Q_1 + Q_2 + Q_3 \qquad\qquad = 1$
$\qquad\qquad Q_i \geqslant 0 \ (i = 1, 2, 3) \ ; \ R_j \qquad \geqslant 0 \ (j = 1, 2) \qquad\qquad (9.26)$

where Q_1, Q_2, Q_3, R_1, R_2 and F are the variables. The solution to (9.26)
is: $Q_1{}^* = Q_2{}^* = 0$, $Q_3{}^* = 1$, $R_1{}^* = R_2{}^* = 1$ and $F^* = 3$. Notice that the
optimal value of F is the same as in the case of weak ranking which
confirms result (9.16). The optimal value of the objective function is
$F^* + \frac{1}{4}R_1{}^* + 1/_8R_2 = 3 + \frac{1}{4} + 1/_8 = 33/_8$.

We see that again the maximin expected return on investment has
increased from 3% to $3^3/_8$%. This is due to the fact that nature's
strategies have been further restricted by the introduction of strict
ranking of probabilities. P_1 must now exceed P_2 by at least $\frac{1}{4}$, and as it
is also the most likely state of nature, share 3 is now even more
attractive than under conditions of weak ranking of probabilities. Thus
it is not surprising that the solution to the problem suggests that the
decision maker should invest all his money in share 3, i.e. adopt pure
strategy 3. The optimal values $R_1{}^* = R_2{}^* = 1$ indicate that if the
minimum differences, $P_1 - P_2 = \frac{1}{4}$ and $P_2 - P_3 = 1/_8$, could each be
increased by a small amount ΔD, say, the optimal expected return would
increase by 1 ΔD in each case. The above interpretations of $R_1{}^*$ and
$R_2{}^*$ are based on the assumption that the small changes ΔD do not affect
the optimal values of $P_j{}^*$ and $Q_i{}^*$. If they do, the linear programmes
(9.25) and (9.26) have to be solved afresh.

It should be stressed that the optimal strategies obtained in cases
(i), (ii) and (iii) are based on the expected value calculations and
that, therefore, they indicate what will be the average return on
investment in the long run, when the investor and hostile nature adopt
their optimal strategies and the same decision problem is faced many
times. The decisions will also be optimal, if the investor selects his
portfolio of shares in the manner indicated above in a large number of
different investment problems. If a single investment decision is taken,
the optimal mixed strategy suggested by the constrained game approach to
decision making may require further consideration if some of the possible
outcomes, however unlikely, are very undesirable. This point may not be
very important in the portfolio selection problem where the optimal
mixed strategy can be literally implemented by buying the optimal mix of
shares. In most decision problems this is not possible, and the optimal
mixed strategy is normally implemented by selecting a pure strategy
according to the probabilities indicated by the optimal mixed strategy.
In such a situation, it is more likely that a single decision may
produce a very low payoff.

Benevolent Nature

So far it was assumed that nature is malevolent, i.e. it consistently
and intelligently acts against the interests of the decision maker. It was

argued in section 9.6 that in classical decision theory nature is usually assumed to play a neutral role, i.e. it neither deliberately hinders nor helps the decision maker. In these conditions it is quite feasible that the decision maker may take an optimistic view of the future and assume that nature will be kind to him. It is natural to assume that such an attitude to nature can be incorporated in the framework of constrained games by assuming that now nature will use the maximin rather than the minimax principle in selecting its optimal strategy. Thus the problem facing nature may now be represented by the following linear programme which incorporates strict ranking of probabilities and is based on result (9.16):

Maximise C

subject to
$$2P_1 + 6P_2 + P_3 - C \geq 0$$
$$P_1 + 2P_2 + 3P_3 - C \geq 0$$
$$4P_1 + 3P_2 + 2P_3 - C \geq 0$$
$$P_1 - P_2 \geq \tfrac{1}{4}$$
$$P_2 - P_3 \geq 1/8$$
$$P_1 + P_2 + P_3 = 1, \quad P_j \geq 0 \quad (j = 1, 2, 3) \qquad (9.27)$$

The solution to this problem is $P_1^* = 13/24$, $P_2^* = 7/24$, $P_3^* = 4/24$ and $C^* = 1\,5/8$. The dual of (9.27) represents the position of the investor and is given by:

Minimise $F - \tfrac{1}{4}R_1 - \tfrac{1}{4}R_2$

subject to
$$2Q_1 + Q_2 + 4Q_3 + R_1 \qquad - F \leq 0$$
$$6Q_1 + 2Q_2 + 3Q_3 - R_1 + R_2 - F \leq 0$$
$$Q_1 + 3Q_2 + 2Q_3 \qquad - R_2 - F \leq 0$$
$$Q_1 + Q_2 + Q_3 \qquad = 1,$$
$$Q_i \geq 0 \ (i = 1, 2, 3) \ ; \quad R_j \geq 0 \ (j = 1, 2) \qquad (9.28)$$

The solution to problem (9.28) is $Q_1^* = 0$, $Q_2^* = 1$, $Q_3^* = 0$, $R_1^* = R_2^* = 1$, and $F^* = 2$, and therefore, the optimal value of the objective function is: $F^* - \tfrac{1}{4}R_1^* - 1/8 R_2^* = 2 - \tfrac{1}{4} - 1/8 = 15/8$, i.e. the same as for the primal.

Thus, in this case, nature is trying to secure a high expected return on investment for the decision maker, but unfortunately, he is working against nature and his own interests and decides to invest all his money in share 2 which yields poor returns under all three states of nature. Given his choice benevolent nature can do no more for him than to secure an expected return of $15/8$. In fact the investor did better for himself when he looked after his own interests, even though nature was hostile to him, for then he secured an expected return of $3 3/8\%$. Thus, as was explained in section 9.6, linear programmes (9.27) and (9.28) do not represent the case of benevolent nature as normally understood, i.e.when the decision maker and nature cooperate, as was assumed, for example, in chapter 3.

When the strict ranking of probabilities incorporated in (9.25) holds and the investor cooperates fully with benevolent nature, the decision problem can be represented correctly by the following quadratic programme which is based on (9.20):

Maximise $\quad Q_1 \; (2P_1 + 6P_2 + P_3) + Q_2 \; (P_1 + 2P_2 + 3P_3) + Q_3 \; (4P_1 + 3P_2 + 2P_2)$

subject to
$$P_1 - P_2 \quad \geqslant \tfrac{1}{4}$$
$$P_2 - P_3 \geqslant 1/8$$
$$P_1 + P_2 + P_3 = 1, \quad P_j \geqslant 0 \quad (j = 1, 2, 3)$$
$$Q_1 + Q_2 + Q_3 = 1, \quad Q_i \geqslant 0 \quad (i = 1, 2, 3) \qquad (9.29)$$

where Q_i and P_j are the variables.

As was explained in section 9.6, the solution to problem (9.29) is given by the pure strategy with the largest maximum expected payoff, i.e. the strategy with the maximax expected payoff. Using the methods developed in section 3.5, we first identify the strategy with the maximax expected payoff when weak ranking of probabilities applies. The partial averages of payoffs for the three strategies are:

$$S_1 : \quad \bar{X}_{11} = 2, \; \bar{X}_{12} = 4, \quad \bar{X}_{13} = 3$$
$$S_2 : \quad \bar{X}_{21} = 1, \; \bar{X}_{22} = 1\tfrac{1}{2}, \; \bar{X}_{23} = 2$$
$$S_3 : \quad \bar{X}_{31} = 4, \; \bar{X}_{32} = 3\tfrac{1}{2}, \; \bar{X}_{33} = 3$$

Since the largest partial average is 4, the maximum expected return on investment is 4% and it occurs when strategy 1 or 3 is selected. When strict ranking of probabilities applies, the maximum expected payoff can be obtained by evaluating result (3.18) for S_1 and S_3:

$$\max E(S_1)_{s.r.} = 4 \; (1 - (1 \times \tfrac{1}{4} + 2 \times 1/8 + 3 \times 0)) + (\tfrac{1}{4} \times 2 + 1/8 \times 8 + 0 \times 9) = 3\tfrac{1}{2}$$
$$\max E(S_3)_{s.r.} = 4 \; (1 - (1 \times \tfrac{1}{4} + 2 \times 1/8 + 3 \times 0 \;) + (\tfrac{1}{4} \times 4 + 1/8 \times 7 + 0 \times 9) = 37/8$$

i.e. the maximax expected payoff is $37/8$%. Notice that although S_1 and S_2 yield the same maximum expected return, 4%, when weak ranking of probabilities applies, S_3 yields a larger maximum, $37/8$, when strict ranking of probabilities holds. This is only to be expected, as strict ranking of probabilities makes N_1 more likely than under conditions of weak ranking, and S_3 is more attractive than S_1 when N_1 occurs. Thus the change in nature's attitude towards the investor has enabled him to increase his expected return on investment by only $\tfrac{1}{2}$%, from $33/8$% to $37/8$%. This shows that strict ranking of probabilities is very restrictive in this example and that the attitude of nature to the decision maker does not matter very much. Finally, it should be noted that if no restrictions were placed on the probabilities of states of nature, the maximum expected return would be 6%. This would happen when the investor selected share 1 and benevolent nature ensured that the second state of nature occurred.

NOTES

(1) We would like to thank M.J. Ryan for suggesting the approach to decision making described in this chapter. However, some of the results and interpretations presented here differ from those given in his 1976 paper.

10   Applications of the methodology in other fields

10.1   INTRODUCTION

The major part of this book has been concerned with the analysis of
decision making in an uncertain environment, intermediate between the
classical extremes characterised as pure risk and pure uncertainty. The
study of decision making, however, embraces a number of other questions,
in some of which ranking procedures also have a potential role. In this
chapter, two further dimensions of decision making are considered. The
first, discussed in section 10.2, is social decision making, and involves
the broadening of Intriligator's well known model of social choice, by
incorporating individuals' preference rankings. The second is multiple-
criteria decision making, where a way of taking into account ranked
weightings of objectives is described and illustrated. This is done in
section 10.3.

10.2   SOCIAL CHOICE AND RANKED INDIVIDUAL PREFERENCES

This section derives from a fusion of concepts in two closely related
areas concerned with decision making. On the one hand, it is based on
the probabilistic social choice model proposed by Intriligator (1973)
and elaborated by Fishburn (1975). On the other, it employs an
optimisation procedure identical in its mathematical foundations to that
developed in chapter 3. The aim is to investigate the maximum and
minimum expected social returns or social costs if choice among a number
of possible actions is made using a lottery-based decision making
technique employing social preferences decided on the basis of
Intriligator's 'average rule' probabilistic social choice model.
However, here, the calculations are made on assumptions which are, in
one important respect, weaker than those employed in the original paper.
It is assumed not that each individual can specify exactly the relative
desirability which he attaches to each possible social action, but only
that he can rank those actions in terms of their desirabilities to him.

Background

In his paper, Intriligator (1973) suggests a re-orientation of the
literature on social choice. He does not look directly at the classical
problems of deriving social preferences or social choice on the basis of
individuals' preferences. Instead, he derives social probabilities of
choosing among alternatives. Implicit in these probabilities is a
social ranking, but it is suggested that social choice will consist not
of the automatic selection of the first-ranked alternative, but will be
based on a random mechanism using the derived social probabilities.
Such an approach has a number of theoretical attractions, for example,
weight is given to the preferences of minorities and to the relative
strength of individual preference. Although direct practical application
is hard to envisage, Fishburn (1975) has provided an interesting
alternative exposition pointing out that the probabilities involved can

equally well be taken to reflect individuals' (and hence society's) vacillation and indecision in the face of actual choices.

Intriligator considers a society of m individuals (i = 1....m) which must choose between n alternatives (j = 1....n). Each individual has a preference among the alternatives which is summarized in an individual probability vector:

$$\underline{q_i} = (q_{i1},....q_{in})$$

$$q_{ij} \geqslant 0 \text{ for all } i \text{ and } j$$

$$\sum_{j=1}^{n} q_{ij} = 1 \text{ for all } i$$

q_{ij} is the probability that individual i would choose alternative j if he could act as 'dictator'.

In Intriligator's model, society selects an alternative by a two-stage process. First, a social probability vector is determined:

$$\underline{p} = (p_1,....p_n)$$

$$p_j \geqslant 0 \text{ for all } j$$

$$\sum_{j=1}^{n} p_j = 1$$

Secondly, the probabilities are input to a random choice mechanism to arrive at the selection of a particular alternative. The p_j are calculated simply as

$$p_j = \frac{1}{m} \sum_{i=1}^{m} q_{ij}.$$

By using this way of deriving the p_j, the social choice model is endowed with a whole series of desirable properties such as collective rationality, unanimity preservation, etc. These are explained fully in Intriligator (1973), pages 554-56. It is also shown there how all these properties are not shared by a number of other well-known social choice rules.

The Problem

Following Intriligator, suppose that a group of m individuals (i = 1....m) must choose one of n possible actions (j = 1....n), A_j. Each individual member of the group may be assumed to have a view as to the desirability from his own standpoint of each of the n actions. Suppose that this view may be summarized by a ranking vector for each individual, i

$$\underline{Q_i} = (q_{i1},....q_{in})$$

where
$$q_{ij} \geqslant 0 \qquad \text{for all } i \text{ and } j \qquad (10.1)$$

$$\sum_{j=1}^{n} q_{ij} = 1 \qquad \text{for all } i \qquad (10.2)$$

$$q_{ij_i} \geqslant q_{ij_i + 1} \quad \text{for all i and } j_i = 1 \ldots n. \tag{10.3}$$

It is assumed that $q_{in + 1} = 0$ to reflect the fact that there are only n actions possible. For each individual, i there is a j_i corresponding to each j, that is each individual has a potentially different ranking of the A_j. The Q_i at this stage merely specify a preference ordering for individual i over the n possible actions. The q_{ij} (equivalently, the q_{ij_i}) which may be interpreted as the probability that individual i would of his own volition choose action $j(j_i)$ are not known or fixed values. It is more reasonable to assume that individuals can rank actions in this way than to believe that they can fix relative weights, q_{ij}, exactly as in Intriligator's original model.

In addition, it is assumed that society as a whole, or some independent arbitrator, is able to attach an unambiguous value, R_j, to the outcome of each of the actions. R_j might, for example, reflect the government's estimate of the net social cost of action j. This valuation may or may not influence the ranking given by each of the m individuals to the actions, and thereby the social preference ranking.

The problem now addressed is whether it is possible to specify maximum and minimum values of the expected social return arising from a choice of one of the n actions which are consistent with the preference rankings of the m decision makers, assuming the use of Intriligator's probabilistic social choice model. It is assumed that the government is unwilling to employ the R_j directly to determine the choice of a course of action. However, used in the way to be described, the R_j estimates enable it to calculate limits on its own evaluation of the expected consequences of a choice undertaken using Intriligator's approach. Furthermore, the question then arises whether, in these circumstances, the extreme expected social returns may be evaluated by any simple method.

The Calculation of Extreme Expected Social Returns

As explained previously, social choice, using Intriligator's model, evolves in two stages. First, a social probability vector, $\underline{p}$, is formed on the basis of the individual probabilities, q_{ij}. $\underline{p} = (p_1, p_2 \ldots p_n)$, where

$$p_j = \frac{1}{m} \sum_{i=1}^{m} q_{ij}.$$

p_j may be regarded as the probability that the social choice will be action j. Secondly, a random lottery-like mechanism, based on the p_j, is used to select which action is to be implemented. Hence, given the R_j social return or social cost valuations defined earlier, the problem of identifying extreme expected social returns (costs) may be defined as

Maximise or Minimise

$$S^* = \sum_{j=1}^{n} p_j R_j$$

Variation in the value of S* arises because the q_{ij} on which the p_j are based are not, as in Intriligator's paper, fixed values, but are free to vary within a range, as specified by the ranking constraints (10.3) in combination with constraints (10.1) and (10.2). Hence the identification of extreme expected social returns is at root a linear programming problem where the objective function is the expression given for S* and the constraints are (10.1), (10.2) and (10.3) on the Q_i' vectors.

Consider the objective function. This may be rewritten as

Maximise or Minimise
$$S^* = \sum_{j=1}^{n} \frac{1}{m} \sum_{i=1}^{m} q_{ij} R_j$$

Now, the optimal solution values of the q_{ij} will not be affected by multiplying the objective function throughout by m and further, the order of summation may be reversed since the function is linear. Hence it is equivalent to seek to

Maximise or Minimise
$$S = \sum_{i=1}^{m} \sum_{j=1}^{n} q_{ij} R_j$$

But this is simply the optimisation of the sum of the expected returns to each of the m individuals, assuming each individual accepts the social evaluation, R_j of the outcome of action j. It should be noted that this is not equivalent to saying that each individual should adopt the social evaluations, R_j. He may continue to have quite different opinions, but, because of the structure of Intriligator's social choice model, the outcome, in the circumstances assumed here, will be equivalent.

Consider now the constraints on the optimisation. It is readily apparent that the constraint set has a pure block diagonal structure since the constraints on the Q_i vectors are specific to individual i and contain no reference to any other member of the decision making group. It may be concluded, therefore, that the optimisation problems concerned with maximising or minimising expected social return subject only to ranking constraints on the relative evaluations placed on the n possible actions by the m decision makers and assuming Intriligator's social choice model are capable of formulation as straightforward linear programming problems where the constraint set is of a particularly simple form. There will, therefore, be no difficulty in determining, in any particular case, the extreme values of S. Indeed, it transpires, as it did in chapter 3, that it is not even necessary to invoke the simplex algorithm to evaluate these extrema.

A Computational Technique

The first step in developing a simple computational technique is to observe that the objective function may be expressed as the sum of m completely separate linear functions

$$\sum_{j=1}^{n} q_{ij} R_j,$$

one for each individual, which coincide exactly with the block diagonal

structure of the constraint set. If each part of the objective function
is totally independent of all other parts of the objective function and
of all parts of the constraint set except its own particular block, then
optimisation of S may be achieved by separately optimising each of the
m constituent parts of the objective function independently and subject
only to their own constraint blocks, and then adding the relevant values
together. Any one of the individual optimisations may be represented
as

<u>Maximise or Minimise</u> $S_i = \sum\limits_{j=1}^{n} q_{ij} R_{ij}$

<u>subject to</u> $\sum\limits_{j=1}^{n} q_{ij} = 1$

$$q_{ij_i} \geqslant q_{ij_i+1} \qquad\qquad (j_i = 1 \ldots n)$$

$$q_{ij} \geqslant 0 \qquad\qquad (j = 1 \ldots n)$$

where, again, there is one j_i corresponding to each j. The distinction
between j and j_i merely reflects the fact that each individual may have
a different preference ranking from the order in which the n actions,
A_j, were initially listed. For ease of exposition, it is best at this
stage to recognise fully this individual ordering by re-writing the
problem in the following way

<u>Maximise or Minimise</u> $S_i = \sum\limits_{j_i=1}^{n} q_{ij_i} R'_{j_i}$

<u>subject to</u> $\sum\limits_{j_i=1}^{n} q_{ij_i} = 1$

$$q_{ij_i} \geqslant q_{ij_i+1} \qquad\qquad (j_i = 1 \ldots n)$$

$$q_{ij_i} \geqslant 0$$

This re-writing ensures that the q_{ij} are re-ordered so that they appear
in the objective function and the first constraint in the decreasing
order of preference implied by the constraints $q_{ij_i} \geqslant q_{ij_i+1}$. In

addition, the R_j are re-ordered to correspond via the R'_{j_i} to this new

ordering of the q_i terms.

This new linear programming problem may be greatly simplified by the
application of the following transformations, which are based on those
developed in chapter 3.

Let $$t_{ij_i} = q_{ij_i} - q_{ij_i+1} \qquad (j_i = 1 \ldots n)$$

Since $t_{in} = q_{in}$ (because $q_{in+1} = 0$), the original constraints now
collapse into just one functional constraint (10.4) and n non-negativity
constraints (10.5).

Secondly, the objective function may be transformed by introducing new variables, Y_{ij_i}, where

$$Y_{ij_i} = \sum_{k=1}^{j_i} R'_{ik} \qquad (j_i = 1 \ldots n)$$

Now
$$S_i = q_{i1}R'_{i1} + \ldots q_{ij_i}R'_{ij_i} + \ldots + q_{in}R'_{in}$$

$$= (t_{i1} + t_{i2} + \ldots t_{in})R'_{i1} + (t_{i2}+t_{i3} +\ldots + t_{in}) R'_{i2}+\ldots+(t_{in}) R'_{in}$$

$$= t_{i1}(R'_{i1}) + t_{i2}(R'_{i1}+R'_{i2}) + \ldots t_{in}(R'_{i1} +\ldots + R'_{in}) = \sum_{j_i=1}^{n} t_{ij_i} Y_{ij_i}$$

Thus the original problem may be re-expressed:

<u>Maximise or Minimize</u>
$$S_i = \sum_{j_i=1}^{n} t_{ij_i} Y_{ij_i}$$

<u>subject to</u>
$$\sum_{j=1}^{n} j_i t_{ij_i} = 1 \qquad\qquad (10.4)$$

$$t_{ij_i} \geqslant 0 \qquad (j_i = 1 \ldots n) \qquad (10.5)$$

Any linear programming problem such as this one, which has just one functional constraint (10.4), will have an optimal solution with only one of the decision variables, t_{ij_i}, positive and all other t_{ij_i} zero.

From constraint (10.5), if only one t_{ij_i} is non-zero, it must equal $1/j_i$.

Substituting into the objective function, it is clear that S_i will be maximised when $\dfrac{Y_{ij_i}}{j_i}$ is maximised and minimized when $\dfrac{Y_{ij_i}}{j_i}$ is minimized.

Hence all that is necessary to calculate the optimal S_i values is to compute the n partial averages

$$S_{ij_i} = 1/j_i\, Y_{ij_i} = \frac{1}{j_i} \sum_{k=1}^{j_i} R'_{ji}.$$

The largest such partial average will be the maximum S_i value and the smallest the minimum.

Maximum and minimum expected social returns (or costs) are found by repeating the partial average calculations for each of the m individuals. Clearly, if some have identical preference rankings, repeated calculation is not necessary. The m maximum S_i values are added together and then divided by m to give the maximum expected social return (cost). Minimum expected social return (cost) is found similarly.

Discussion

Thus Intriligator's probabilistic model of social choice can also be applied in situations where the decision makers' preferences between actions cannot be specified in terms of exact values, q_{ij}, but only as a ranking of these actions. In such a situation, provided some exogeneous form of social evaluation, R_j, is available for each action, it is possible to predict the limits within which the expected social return arising from a decision made by a group of decision makers using Intriligator's average rule will be. This is a much more reasonable proposition than attempting to find just a single expected social return figure based on the assumption of fixed q_{ij} values, and adds a valuable degree of freedom in the potential application of Intriligator's original technique.

10.3 MULTIPLE OBJECTIVE DECISION MAKING WITH RANKED CRITERIA

Background

The second example of the use of methodology similar to that developed in chapter 3 is concerned with multiple criteria decision making. In recent years an increasing number of papers has been appearing concerned both with the theory and practice of multiple criteria decision making. French and Dutch authors in particular have made significant contributions. The majority of early formal work on multiple criteria decision making appears to have emanated from the United States and to be attributable to psychologists and management scientists. However, many of the techniques derived are far from being restricted in their application to single subjects, and many other potential areas of application exist. For example, public policy decisions frequently involve the consideration of a wide range of consequences which affect many different groups of people in different places and in different ways.

A Maximin/Maximax Weighted Evaluation Approach to Multiple Criteria Decision Making

Many questions of public policy have to be answered in the face of two major problems. These are, firstly, uncertainty and, secondly, the difficulty, if not impossibility of unambiguously mapping the multidimensional descriptions of the consequences of alternative policies on to a single ordinal scale. The use of formal methods rather than a purely subjective ranking of alternatives cannot totally overcome the difficulties caused by these two factors. It does, however, have some value. Formalisation can help clarify both what is being aimed at and the relative importance of conflicting goals. Furthermore, communication with other decision makers and with members of the public is facilitated if some framework for presenting and comparing the consequences of different courses of action exists.

   Even if it may ultimately be possible to develop a single strategy for handling simultaneously the twin problems of uncertainty and multiple criteria, current practice is nowhere near this point. This section, therefore, concentrates on the formal assessment of preferences in the presence of multiple criteria. It ignores the problem of uncertainty. What will be presented is a new formal technique for comparing different courses of action. Its principal recommendations are simplicity of application, the use of an ordinal rather than a cardinal scale for assessing the relative importance of different criteria, and comparison based on the performance of each alternative policy relative to the performance of all other possibilities for each individual criterion.

It should, however, be emphasised that there is no single multiple criteria technique which is unambiguously superior to all others. The most appropriate method, or indeed, combination of methods, will vary from problem to problem. The ultimate need is to develop a strategy for presenting all those potential courses of action which might reasonably be regarded as attractive without obscuring what is at best likely to be a complex decision by the presence of many less desirable possibilities.

The best known methods for reducing multiple consequences to a single dimension are, of course, straightforward financial appraisal and cost-benefit analysis. In the former case, market prices are used to evaluate the different consequences of a course of action. In the latter account is taken of consequences which may not have a market and for which shadow prices have to be estimated. The criticisms of cost-benefit analysis and related techniques are well documented, see, for example, Nijkamp (1975), pp. 89-91, for a brief summary. They need not be recounted here. Essentially, however, the problem is that in reducing the multiple dimensional consequences of an act to a single dimensional evaluation, information is inevitably lost. If there is no doubt about the rates at which decision makers are prepared to trade off different consequences against each other at all different levels of attainment of those consequences, then reduction to a single dimension should cause no great problem. If, however, as is very likely, this is not the case, then two major techniques of multiple criteria analysis immediately gain importance. One of these is the comparison and ranking of strategies on the basis of more than one dimension of decision. The other is the reduction of the dimensionality of the problem by fixing acceptable weights to the different consequences of strategies and the exploration of the implications of some tolerance in the precise values of those weights. In almost all cases of any complexity the second will be an essential component of any evaluation strategy.

Thus, using the notation of Keeney and Raiffa (1976), the typical situation is to be faced with a set of feasible policy choices (acts) (1) , A, with individual members, a. With each a, which is a member of set A is associated an n-tuple, $X = (X_1, \ldots, X_n)$ of evaluators of each act, a. This n-tuple maps the act, into n-dimensional consequence space. X may be regarded as a vector of attributes. Although some (relatively weak) methods exist for ranking different X vectors while they are still in vector form, the principal concern must be with techniques for collapsing the $X_1, \ldots, X_n$ into a scalar index of value, using a function defined on consequence space such that

$$v(X_1, \ldots, X_n) \geqslant v(X_1', \ldots, X_n') \Leftrightarrow (X_1, \ldots, X_n) \succcurlyeq (X_1', \ldots, X_n')$$

or, equivalently, $a \succcurlyeq a'$. $\succcurlyeq$ represents weak preference. Throughout this section it is assumed that high levels of the value function are preferable, i.e., that "highest" is synonymous with "best".

MacCrimmon (1973) provides a valuable survey of multiple criteria decision making models, identifying four major categories, (a)Weighting Methods; (b)Sequential Elimination Methods; (c)Mathematical Programming Methods and (d)Spatial Proximity Methods. Here, concentration will be focussed on (a), which involves the construction of a scalar index of value, $v(X_1, \ldots, X_n)$, by associating a weight with each attribute,

aggregating the weighted individual measures and selecting the
alternative with the highest weighted sum. In particular, just one type
of weighting method will be explored. At one point or another, a
weighting method is central to the evaluation procedure of most practical
multiple criteria decision making models. The main difference between
methods lies in the techniques used for establishing the weights.

A very simplistic, but, on occasions, useful weighting scheme uses
ideas from the field of decision making under uncertainty described in
chapter 2, viz., maximin and maximax. In the maximax case, for each
possible strategy, a weight of one is given to the consequence recording
the highest score for that strategy. A maximax choice then selects that
strategy which has the highest maximum level of achievement in terms of
all the consequences considered. Maximin strategy choice is defined
analogously.

The technique to be presented now is a generalisation of the basic
maximin/maximax weighting scheme. Maximin analysis in its pure form will
be appropriate when,for technical or political reasons, an act will be
assessed in terms of the weakest link in the chain. That is, evaluation
will depend on its performance in the dimension in which it performs
most poorly. Maximax can be applied when the system under examination
is sufficiently flexible in its operation that, after its implementation,
it may be used in such a way as to exploit the particularly outstanding
level of achievement of the consequence for which it was chosen. For
example, in public policy choice, it may well be desirable to favour
acts which are relatively unlikely to encourage opposition by certain
lobbying groups. Maximin choice will select policies which avoid unduly
poor performances in terms of any single criterion and so will reduce the
probability of causing major offence to any influence group.

In its basic form, however, maximin/maximax analysis is open to three
significant objections:
   (a)it assumes that the scales on which the different attributes are
      measured are directly comparable;
   (b)it ignores all consequences of each act except the very worst in
      the maximin case or the very best in maximax;
   (c)it ignores any relative importance that the decision maker may wish
      to place on different attributes.

Consider, initially, the first objection. Frequently, a plausible
objective on the part of the decision maker will be to avoid strategies
for which any criterion score is significantly lower than that achieved
by other strategies for that criterion. Such an attitude may be
incorporated, and the problem of comparability handled by first
standardising each set of criterion scores across all available
strategies by subtracting the mean score for that criterion, and then
dividing by its standard deviation. This is close in spirit to the
normalisation used in concordance analysis, see, e.g. Nijkamp (1975),
p. 95. Alternatively, if comparability is not a problem, but it is still
desired to avoid poor relative performances, a regret matrix may be
computed in the normal way and, for example, a minimax weighted regret
strategy sought.

Objections (b) and (c) above may be handled in the following way.
Consider the maximin case, since maximax follows by direct analogy.

Suppose, instead of giving a weight of one to the worst (standardised) outcome of each strategy and one of zero to all others, that, taking into account the standardisation that has taken place, the decision maker weights relative achievement according to the different criteria (j = 1....n) with non-negative weights, w_j, where, without loss of generality, it is assumed that $\sum_{j=1}^{n} w_j = 1$. Further, assume that these weights are not known quantities, but merely reflect a ranking of the importance of the criteria, $w_1 \geqslant w_1 \geqslant \ldots \geqslant w_n$. It may now be shown that it is possible to calculate extreme values of the sum of the weighted individual criteria values, which are consistent with the decision maker's ranking. By comparing minima across strategies (in the maximin case) an optimal strategy may be selected.

The ranking of criteria, rather than the establishment of exact weights, is a sensible way of incorporating a view of the relative importance of different consequences without at the same time imputing too much reliability to the means by which the decision maker's attitudes to the consequences were established. This approach has been employed usefully by French and Dutch authors, e.g. Guijou (1971), Nijkamp (1975).

For simplicity, consider the problem of determining the extreme weighted evaluations, W, for a single strategy, with criterion scores S_j (j = 1....n), where S_j is the standardised score of the strategy for criterion j. Adopting the approach used in earlier chapters in the context of decision making under uncertainty, the problem may be formalised as a pair of linear programming problems:

<u>Maximise or Minimise</u> $W = \sum_{j=1}^{n} w_j S_j$

<u>subject to</u> $\sum_{j=1}^{n} w_j = 1$ (10.6)

$w_j - w_{j+1} \geqslant 0$ (j = 1....(n-1))   (10.7)

$w_j \geqslant 0$ (j = 1....n)   (10.8)

The problem may be simplified greatly by the application of the now familiar transformations:

$v_j = w_j - w_{j+1}$ (j = 1....(n-1))

$Y_j = \sum_{k=1}^{j} S_k$ (j = 1....n)

$v_n = w_n$ (since $w_{n+1} = 0$) and so the original constraints (10.6) and (10.7) collapse into just one functional constraint, (10.9) and n non-negativity constraints, (10.10). Further, since $w_j = \sum_{k=j}^{n} v_k$, and given that (10.10) holds, then the non-negativity constraints (10.8) are also obeyed. Therefore, the original problem may be re-expressed:

<u>Maximise or Minimise</u>

$$W = \sum_{j=1}^{n} v_j Y_j$$

<u>subject to</u>

$$\sum_{j=1}^{n} j v_j = 1 \qquad\qquad (10.9)$$

$$v_j \geq 0 \qquad j = 1 \ldots n \qquad (10.10)$$

A linear programming problem of this type, with only one functional constraint, will again have an optimal solution with just one of the decision variables, v_j, positive and all other v_j zero. From (10.9), if only one v_j is non-zero, its value must be $1/j$. Thus the objective function will be maximised when Y_j/j is maximised and minimised when Y_j/j is minimised. To identify maximum and minimum values of W, all that is necessary is to calculate all partial sums $W_j = 1/j \sum_{k=1}^{j} S_k$ and locate the extreme values. Strategy choice is then simply a matter of comparing weighted minima across strategies and selecting that policy with the maximum minimum score. A numerical example will be given in the next sub-section.

Two forms of extension of the basic results are possible, both concerned with assessing the sensitivity of the extreme weighted evaluations just determined. In its basic form, the technique uses only one extreme weighting per strategy to evaluate that strategy. It does not give any information about how the weighted evaluation will vary if an actual weighting, still consistent with the given ranking of criteria, but not the extreme possibility, were in fact employed. In practice, therefore, a decision maker might give some additional value to a strategy whose evaluation was relatively insensitive to a departure from the extreme set of weights actually used for the strategy's evaluation. It could be regarded as more reliable than strategies with similar extreme weighted scores, but of greater sensitivity. Such a strategy would then be relatively secure against the argument that the weighted extreme was based on a weighting 0.5, 0.5, 0, 0 whereas, in some critic's judgement, the correct weighting should be 0.4, 0.3, 0.15, 0.15.

An index of strategy sensitivity to consistent but non-extreme weightings is the maximum weighted squared deviation about a weighted evaluation which can be attained. This indicator is derived by analogy with the variance index of deviation about a mean, since $\sum_{j=1}^{n} w_j = 1$. The lower is this maximum, the more reliable the strategy may be held to be.

The maximum weighted squared deviation indicator can be computed by a series of simple arithmetic steps. As is shown in chapter 4, all that is required is to compute a series of partial variances,

$$1/j \sum_{k=1}^{j} S_k^2 - (1/j \sum_{k=1}^{j} S_k)^2, \text{ for } j = 1 \ldots n.$$

The maximum such partial sum gives the value of the required indicator. Depending on the value judgements of the decision maker, sensitivity measured in this way, may be traded off against the extreme W figure obtained from the linear programming analysis.

A second approach to sensitivity testing is to examine changes in the
W index as a result of changes in the ranking of criteria or of the
introduction of new criteria. This question has been examined from the
point of view of decision making under uncertainty in chapter 6. If a
major perturbation in the ranking of criteria occurs, then it is probably
simplest to recompute all the partial sums from scratch. If however,
the ranking change consists only of the inversion of two criteria, say
those previously ranked g and h, where $1 \leqslant g < h \leqslant n$, then the partial sums
which will change are $W_g \dots W_{k-1}$. These change to $W'_j = W_j + {}^1/_j (S_h - S_g)$
for $j = g \dots (h-1)$. All these new partial averages will have to be
compared with those unaffected by the inversion in order to locate the
new extrema.

If a new criterion is introduced, ranked in the gth. position, then
again, it is not necessary to perform an entire calculation of partial
sums again. Partial sums $W_1 \dots W_{g-1}$ will be unchanged. All
subsequent partial sums will change as follows

$$W'_k = W_k + \frac{1}{k} (S_N - S_k) \qquad k = g \dots n$$

$$W'_{n+1} = \frac{1}{n+1} (S_1 + \dots + S_{g-1} + S_N + S_g + \dots + S_n)$$

where S_N is the standardised score of this strategy on the new
criterion. New extrema are located by inspection of all (n+1) results.
Other sensitivity analyses, for example, for changes in the S_i, are
possible. The calculations simply parallel those of chapter 6.

A Numerical Example

In this section, a brief numerical example is given. It is based on one
in van Delft and Nijkamp (1976), pp. 51 - 55, which involved five
possible plans assessed on the basis of ten different criteria. The
plans refer to different development schemes for a new industrial area
near Rotterdam. The criteria are such as value added per hectare,
demand for labour, environmental quality, proportion of foreign
labourers employed, etc. The normalised plan impact matrix they give on
page 54 has been transformed to a standardised plan impact matrix, as
shown here in Table 10.1, using the relationship between normalised and

Criterion	Plan Number				
	1	2	3	4	5
1	-0.516	-0.476	0.262	0.665	0.065
2	0.641	0.165	0.165	-0.663	-0.307
3	-0.457	-0.418	0.026	0.781	0.067
4	-0.909	0.600	0.199	-0.011	0.122
5	-0.527	0.791	-0.011	-0.183	-0.069
6	-0.923	0.231	0.103	0.359	0.231
7	0.597	0.357	-0.021	-0.673	-0.261
8	0.673	-0.007	-0.040	0.027	-0.653
9	0.332	0.409	-0.260	-0.279	-0.202
10	0.061	0.832	-0.528	-0.557	0.192

Table 10.1 The Standardised Plan Impact Matrix

standardised scores developed in Pearman (1979). Further, four rankings of criteria, A, B, C and D have been considered. These are consistent with the preference scores 2, 3, 4 and 5 on page 55 of van Delft and Nijkamp. Where equal preference scores were originally given, an arbitrary ranking has been imposed, although, with the technique developed here, the possibility of some equal weighting is not excluded. The four rankings are shown in Table 10.2.

Criterion	Ranking			
	A	B	C	D
1	7	2	5	6
2	10	9	3	4
3	6	7	8	9
4	1	4	2	2
5	3	5	4	3
6	5	6	6	5
7	9	8	1	1
8	2	3	10	8
9	8	10	7	7
10	4	1	9	10

Table 10.2 The Four Rankings Examined

The first step is to compute all partial sums and thus find the extreme weighted evaluations for each plan. These calculations are shown fully for Ranking A in Table 10.3:

Plan j=	1	2	3	4	5	6	7	8	9	10
1	-0.91	-0.12	-0.25	-0.18	-0.33	-0.35	-0.37	-0.28	-0.19	-0.10
2	0.60	0.30	0.46	0.55	0.49	0.34	0.22	0.22	0.26	0.25
3	0.20	0.08	0.05	-0.10	-0.06	-0.04	0.00	-0.03	-0.03	-0.01
4	-0.01	0.01	-0.06	-0.18	-0.07	0.07	0.15	0.10	0.01	-0.05
5	0.12	-0.27	-0.20	-0.10	-0.08	-0.02	-0.01	-0.03	-0.06	-0.08

Plan No.	1	2	3	4	5
Minimum Value	-0.91	0.22	-0.10	-0.18	-0.27
Maximum Value	-0.10	0.60	0.20	0.15	0.12

Table 10.3 Partial Sum Calculations for Ranking A

and in summary form for the remaining rankings in Table 10.4. The main conclusion which can be reached in this example, either using maximin or maximax strategy choice, is that Plan 2 clearly dominates all others over quite a wide range of weight rankings. This is in line with the conclusion of van Delft and Nijkamp, who used a concordance analysis coupled with an analysis of dominance.

	Ranking	B	C	D
Plan 1	Minimum	-0.37	-0.27	-0.28
	Maximum	0.07	0.59	0.59
Plan 2	Minimum	0.12	0.21	0.18
	Maximum	0.83	0.48	0.48
Plan 3	Minimum	-0.53	-0.02	-0.02
	Maximum	0.02	0.12	0.12
Plan 4	Minimum	-0.56	-0.67	-0.67
	Maximum	0.15	0.00	0.00
Plan 5	Minimum	-0.13	-0.26	-0.26
	Maximum	0.19	-0.04	-0.04

Table 10.4 Extreme Weighted Evaluations, for Rankings B, C and D

Given the performance of Plan 2, it is unlikely that any sensitivity information would be required in this case. However, for purposes of illustration, Table 10.5 shows, for the first ranking only, the calculation of the maximum weighted squared deviation measure described earlier, and Table 10.6 shows the effect of reversing the third and fifth ranked criteria, again in Ranking A, so that the order of criteria is 4, 8, 6, 10, 5....

Plan	$j=$ 1	2	3	4	5	6	7	8	9	10	Maximum
1	0.00	0.63	0.46	0.36	0.37	0.32	0.28	0.30	0.34	0.37	0.63
2	0.00	0.09	0.12	0.12	0.11	0.20	0.26	0.24	0.20	0.18	0.26
3	0.00	0.02	0.01	0.07	0.06	0.05	0.06	0.06	0.05	0.05	0.07
4	0.00	0.00	0.01	0.05	0.09	0.18	0.20	0.19	0.23	0.25	0.25
5	0.00	0.15	0.11	0.11	0.10	0.09	0.08	0.07	0.07	0.07	0.15

Table 10.5 Partial Squared Deviation Calculations for Ranking A

Plan	Old Minimum	New Minimum	Old Maximum	New Maximum
1	*	*	*	*
2	*	*	*	*
3	-0.10	-0.06	*	*
4	-0.18	-0.07	*	*
5	*	*	*	*

* No change as a result of new ranking.

Table 10.6 Effect of Changed Ranking on the Extreme Weighted Evaluation

The maximum variance measure tends to support the claim of Plan 3 to be the second best option available. However, as Table 10.6 shows, should there be a change of opinion about the ranking such as to reverse the third and fifth ranked criteria, then the position of Plan 3 is much less secure as runner up, and it might well be desirable to consider the claims of Plan 4.

Summary

The extent to which it is feasible or necessary to approach the full range of public sector decision problems from the multiple criteria point of view is a matter which deserves fuller consideration. For the present, however, there is little doubt that policy choice at the final stages can often benefit from this type of approach. The new technique put forward in this section represents an extension of existing methods. While limited in the types of choice to which it can be applied, its simplicity makes it potentially valuable for presenting a series of solutions to final decision makers, on the basis of a clear ranking of criteria and in such a way that the effects of changes in the basis of the original calculations can readily be made and their effects demonstrated. The departure which this technique and others related to it suggest from current common practice is not an absolute one. It lies in the relatively greater concentration it gives to the presentation of sets of good solutions rather than of a single optimal outcome, and in its emphasis on the tentative understanding which exists of the trade-offs between many important consequences. It encourages those concerned with decisions to face firmly awkward, qualitative assessments which might otherwise wrongly be excluded from consideration. It promotes the exploration of the implications of changes in rankings, etc. It is this exploratory aspect as much as anything which is the main potential contribution of multiple criteria decision making.

NOTES

(1) In this section, acts, strategies and courses of action will be used interchangeably, unlike, for example, Fishburn (1964).

11 Conclusions

The starting point for this book was the observation that there exist
many practical decision problems intermediate between the classical
extremes of decision making under uncertainty and decision making under
risk. Although most of the examples given in earlier chapters are taken
from applications in the fields of economics and management, the problem
is a general one. There are many circumstances in which the amount of
information available to a decision maker does not permit the precise
specification of the probabilities of future states of nature, but where
the assumption of complete ignorance conditions is obviously
unreasonable. If the available information can be specified in some way,
and appropriately utilised, the quality of decision making will be
improved. We have attempted to show that a very effective way of
formally characterising the existence of incomplete knowledge of
probabilities of states of nature is to assume that the decision maker
is able to specify a ranking of the probabilities. Given such an
assumption, the preceding chapters have demonstrated how a number of
operational techniques for guiding decision making may be developed.

The most important results are those given in chapter 3 and, later, in
chapter 9. In chapter 3 it was shown that both for a strict and a weak
ranking of probabilities of states of nature, it is possible to derive,
in a very straightforward manner, maximum and minimum expected values of
the payoffs of a strategy. Moreover, it was also shown that a decision
maker who employs these values to guide his choice between strategies,
rather than relying on pure maximum and minimum payoffs will, over a
series of problems, make better decisions. This is because the extreme
expected value methods take full advantage of all the information
available to the decision maker. Chapter 4 showed that the maximum
variance of a strategy can also be computed by a simple procedure, and
this may be interpreted as a measure of the risk that a strategy will
not yield a payoff close to its expected value. As such it may be used
as a further guide to the selection of a strategy. Chapter 5 explored
how variance and expected value of payoffs might be traded off against
each other in conditions of incomplete knowledge.

A number of extensions of the basic results were discussed in chapters
6, 7 and 8. The sensitivity analysis of chapter 6 is particularly
important for practical decision making, since, in the real world, the
parameters of any problem are themselves liable to be uncertain. For
the same reason, the ability to update a probability ranking in the light
of evidence of previous outcomes, as discussed in chapter 7, is also of
potential practical value. The development of the concept of weak
statistical dominance enabled the decision maker to take a different view
of strategy choice. It emphasised the important role that pairwise
comparison of strategies frequently has. It was also shown that there is
a close connection between weak statistical dominance and the long-
established concept of 'regret' or opportunity cost in decision making.

Chapter 9 is the second key chapter in the book. In it, the decision maker's problem was reformulated as a constrained game against nature, and this, apart from embedding the problem in an elegant and more general framework, permitted the determination of optimal <u>mixed</u> strategies which the decision maker could adopt against a hostile nature. Strict ranking of the probabilities of the states of nature was used in the formulation of the constrained game, and it was possible to show that many of the maximin results developed in chapter 3 can be regarded as special cases of the more general game theory formulation.

Chapter 10 illustrated adaptations of the basic methodology of chapter 3 to two other problems where the assumption of a ranking constraint was of potential value in extending existing models. One application was to social choice theory, the other to multiple criteria decision making. It seems likely that similar extensions of the methodology will be possible in other areas, and this remains an interesting area for further research. Similarly, the game theory approach of chapter 9 looks to have a ready application to portfolio selection where a defensive strategy is required. The basic decision making approach described in the book could be applied in the field of investment decision making, both private and public. Such empirical work looks very promising, and would provide a valuable test for the theory.

Finally, it is worth mentioning that a number of theoretical developments, not fully examined in earlier chapters, are the subject of active current research. Of these the most notable is the extension of the results outlined in chapters 4, 5, 6, 7 and 8 to incorporate strict as well as weak ranking, a development which will further generalise the established results.

Bibliography

Agunwamba, C.C., Decision theory under uncertainty and expected
    probability distribution , paper presented to the 5th symposium on
    Operations Research, University of Cologne, West Germany, 1980.
Agunwamba, C.C., 'On decision theory and incomplete knowledge', Journal
    of Management Studies, vol. 18, No. 1, 1981.
Allais, M., Fondements d'une théorie positive des choix comportant un
    risque et critique des postulats et axiomes de l'école américaine,
    Imprimerie Nationale, Paris, 1955.
Arrow, K.J., Essays in the theory of risk-bearing, North-Holland
    Publishing Co., Amsterdam, 1970.
Baumol, W.J., Economic theory and operations analysis, 3rd edition,
    Prentice Hall, Englewood Cliffs, New Jersey, 1972.
Cannon, C.M. and Kmietowicz, Z.W., 'Decision theory and incomplete
    knowledge', Journal of Management Studies, vol. 11, No. 3, 1974.
Charnes, A. and Cooper, W.W., Management models and industrial
    applications of linear programming, vol. 2, J. Wiley, New York, 1961.
De Groot, M.H., Optimal statistical decisions, McGraw-Hill, New York,
    1970.
Fishburn, P.C., Decision and value theory, J. Wiley, New York, 1964.
Fishburn, P.C., 'Alternative axiomatizations of one-way expected
    utility', Annals of Mathematical Statistics, vol. 43, 1972.
Fishburn, P.C., 'A probabilistic model of social choice : comment',
    Review of Economic Studies, vol. 42, 1975.
Fishburn, P.C., 'Utility independence on subsets of product sets',
    Operations Research, vol. 24, 1976.
Fishburn, P.C., 'Multiattribute utilities in expected utility theory'
    in Bell, D.E., Keeney, R.L. and Raiffa, H. (eds) Conflicting
    objectives in decisions, J. Wiley, New York, 1977.
Fisher, I.N. and Hall, G.R., 'Risk and corporate rates of return',
    Quarterly Journal of Economics, vol. 83, 1969.
Guijou, J.L., 'On French location models for production units', Regional
    and Urban Economics, vol. 1, 1971.
Hampton, J.M., Moore, P.G. and Thomas, H., 'Subjective probability and
    its measurement', Journal of the Royal Statistical Society, Series A,
    vol. 136, 1973.
Hey, J.D., Uncertainty in microeconomics, Martin Robertson, Oxford,1979.
Hillier, F.S. and Lieberman, G.J., Introduction to operations research,
    2nd edition, Holden-Day, San Francisco, 1974.
Intriligator, M.D., 'A probabilistic model of social choice', Review of
    Economic Studies, vol. 40, 1973.
Keeney, R.L. and Raiffa, H., Decisions with multiple objectives :
    preferences and value trade-offs, J. Wiley, New York, 1976.
Kmietowicz, Z.W. and Pearman, A.D., 'Decision theory and incomplete
    knowledge : maximum variance', Journal of Management Studies, vol. 13,
    No. 2, 1976.
Kmietowicz, Z.W. and Pearman, A.D., 'Decision theory and ranked
    probabilities', in van Dam, C. (ed) Trends in financial decision
    making : planning and capital investment decisions, Martinus Nijhoff,
    Leiden, 1978.

Kmietowicz, Z.W. and Pearman, A.D., 'Decision theory and incomplete knowledge : Bayesian estimation, probability matrix and entropy', Bedrijfskunde, vol. 51, No. 3, 1979.

Kmietowicz, Z.W. and Pearman, A.D., 'Decision theory and weak statistical dominance', Journal of the Operational Research Society, vol. 30, No. 12, 1979.

Kmietowicz, Z.W. and Pearman, A.D., 'Decision theory, ranked probabilities and weak statistical dominance', Proceedings of the 14th Annual Conference on Statistics, Computer Science and Operations Research, vol. 2,, Cairo University Press, 1979.

Kmietowicz, Z.W. and Pearman, A.D.,'Decision theory, ranked probabilities and statistical dominance', Operations Research Verfahren, vol. 34, 1979.

Knight, F.H., Risk, uncertainty and profit, Houghton Mifflin, Boston, 1921.

Luce, R.D., 'Semiorders and a theory of utility discrimination', Econometrica, vol. 24, 1956.

Luce, R.D. and Raiffa, H., Games and decisions : introduction and critical survey, J. Wiley, New York, 1957.

MacCrimmon, K.R., 'An overview of multiple objective decision making', in Cochrane, J.L. and Zeleny, M. (eds), Multiple criteria decision making, University of South Carolina Press, Columbia, South Carolina, 1973.

Markowitz, H.M., Portfolio selection : efficient diversification of investment, J. Wiley, New York, 1959.

Moore, P.G., and Thomas, H., 'Measuring uncertainty', Omega, vol. 3, 1975.

Nijkamp, P., 'A multicriteria analysis for project evaluation : economic - ecological evaluation of a land reclamation project', Papers of the Regional Science Association, vol. 35, 1975.

Pearman, A.D., 'Transport investment appraisal in the presence of uncertainty', Transportation Research, vol. 10, 1976.

Pearman, A.D., 'A weighted maximin and maximax approach to multiple criteria decision making', Operational Research Quarterly, vol. 28, 1977.

Pearman, A.D., 'Problems of optimising investments in road networks', in Bonsall, P.W., Dalvi, M.Q. and Hills, P.J., (eds) Urban transportation planning, Abacus Press, Tunbridge Wells, 1977.

Pearman, A.D., 'Uncertainty and the transport investment decision', in Visser, E.J. (ed), Transport decisions in an age of uncertainty, Martinus Nijhoff, Leiden, 1977.

Pearman, A.D., 'A weighted maximin and maximax approach to multiple criteria decision making : a reply', Journal of the Operational Research Society, vol. 29, No. 6, 1978.

Pearman, A.D., 'Approaches to multiple objective decision making with ranked criteria', in Cullen, I.(ed), Analysis and decision in regional planning, Pion, London, 1979.

Pearman, A.D. and Kmietowicz, Z.W., 'Decision theory and incomplete knowledge : sensitivity analysis', University of Leeds School of Economic Studies Discussion Paper Series, No. 40, 1976.

Pearman, A.D. and Kmietowicz, Z.W., 'Social choice and ranked individual preferences', Bulletin of Economic Research, vol. 32, 1980.

Pratt, J.W., Raiffa, H. and Schlaiffer, R., Introduction to statistical decision theory, McGraw-Hill, New York, 1965.

Raiffa, H., Decision Analysis, Addison-Wesley, Reading, Massachusetts, 1968.

Roberts, B. and Schulze, D.L., Modern mathematics and economic analysis, W.W.Norton, New York, 1973.

Ryan, M.J., 'Decision theory, incomplete knowledge and constrained games', Hull Economic Research Papers, No. 14, 1976.

Savage, L.J., Foundations of statistics, J. Wiley, New York, 1954.

Slovic, P. and Tversky, A., 'Who accepts Savage's axiom?', Behavioural Science, vol. 19, 1974.

Starr, M.K., 'Reducing the uncertainty of the future', in van Dam, C. (ed) Trends in financial decision making : planning and capital investment decisions, Martinus Nijhoff, Leiden, 1978.

Thrall, R.M., 'Applications of multidimensional utility theory', in Thrall, R.M., Coombs, C.H. and Davis, R.L., (eds) Decision processes, J. Wiley, New York, 1954.

Vajda, S., Mathematical programming, Addison-Wesley, London, 1961.

van Delft, A. and Nijkamp, P., Multicriteria analysis and regional decision making, Martinus Nijhoff, Leiden, 1977.

von Neumann, J. and Morgenstern, O., Theory of games and economic behaviour, Princeton University Press, Princeton, New Jersey, 1947.

Whitmore, G.A. and Findlay, M.C., (eds) Stochastic dominance, Lexington Books, Lexington, Massachusetts, 1978.

Author index

Subject index